MORE THAN A CHAMPION

MORE THAN A CHAMPION

The Style of Muhammad Ali

*JAN
PHILIPP
REEMTSMA*

*Translated from
the German by*
JOHN E. WOODS

Alfred A. Knopf   New York   1998

This Is a Borzoi Book
Published by Alfred A. Knopf, Inc.

Copyright © 1998 by Alfred A. Knopf, Inc.
All rights reserved under International and Pan-
American Copyright Conventions. Published in the
United States by Alfred A. Knopf, Inc., New York,
and simultaneously in Canada by Random House of
Canada Limited, Toronto. Distributed by Random
House, Inc., New York.

www.randomhouse.com

Originally published in Germany as *Mehr als ein
Champion* by Klett-Cotta, Stuttgart, in 1995.
Copyright © 1995 by J. G. Cotta'sche
Buchhandlung Nachfolger GmbH

Owing to limitations of space, all acknowledgments
for permission to reprint previously published
material may be found on page 173.

Library of Congress Cataloging-in-Publication Data
Reemtsma, Jan Philipp.
[Mehr als ein Champion. English]
More than a champion: the style of Muhammad Ali /
Jan Philipp Reemtsma ; translated by John E. Woods. —
1st American ed.
p.   cm.
"This is a Borzoi book"—T.p. verso.
Includes bibliographical references (p.   ).
ISBN 0-375-40030-3
1. Ali, Muhammad, 1942–   .   2. Boxers (Sports)—
United States—Psychology.   3. Boxing—Social
aspects—United States.   I. Title.
GV1132.A44R4413 1998
796.83'092—dc21
[B]   97-36675   CIP

Manufactured in the United States of America
First American Edition

For Johann Scheerer.
And for all the others who
also wanted this book.

Contents

MORE THAN A CHAMPION

PROLOGUE

Manila, 1 October 1975; Muhammad Ali vs. Joe Frazier. Bell for the first round. A few steps bring the two boxers to the center of the ring. Muhammad Ali holds both fists almost level with his eyes; below his shoulders the body is turned a little to the right of its vertical axis, the left leg advanced and slightly bent at the knee, the right stretched backward, the way a fencer would hold his body for a lunge. Both fists, however, are approximately the same distance from his opponent. This is Ali's way of offering the smallest possible area to body blows from Joe Frazier, the smaller man, while at the same time retaining for himself the possibility of attacking with either his left or his right. Frazier stands bent forward, holding his gloves at chest level, tapping them together as if eager to go to work. Ali will attack with jabs, will try to hit Frazier's head and make the most of his longer reach. Frazier will try to dodge under the jabs and either hit Ali low in the ribs or land a left or right hook higher up. It is the third time that Ali and Frazier have faced each other in the ring.

Do I dare write like this without any sort of mental reservation? Across from me, the television; next to it, a pile of about twenty videos—*Ali versus Frazier, The Third and Final Fight*—*The Thriller in Manila, Best of the Muhammad Ali/Ken Norton Trilogy, The Muhammad Ali Story, The Jack Johnson Story, Heavyweights,* and so on; to my left, beside my laptop, the remote with a slow-motion dial; on the desk, books with titles like *Muhammad Ali: His Life and Times, The Greatest: My Own Story, Heavyweight Champions, Classic Moments of Boxing, The Great Fights: A Pictorial History of Boxing's Greatest Bouts,* yes, and some classics, too—Mailer, Oates, London, Hemingway.

I don't want the woman or man who reads this to misunderstand me. Especially since I would not like to call those last two authors as witnesses—their glorification of pure atavism is annoying. Whatever Huizinga may say, human beings do not first become human at play, and a man is not particularly human when he lets someone batter his head. A fascination with boxing is not Döblin's or Brecht's most interesting aspect. And I find the evocation of the archaic element inappropriate as well, at least when I am sitting in front of the television at four in the morning to watch a satellite broadcast of a boxing match. On the other hand, no other event on TV can bring me to set my alarm for 4:00 a.m.

Should I try to track down the motives for such behavior? And if I found them, should I own up to what I've discovered? I fear that whatever I might have to say would not erase traces of mockery in the smile of any woman who reads this (should there be one), nor can I fend off the shrugs of those readers who were not sitting in front of their television screens at 4:00 a.m. that morning. But those people watching on tenterhooks, as I was, furious with German commentators who, for starters, had to unload their steady barrage of "Cassius Clay alias Muhammad Ali" (an effrontery they would never have allowed themselves in the case of a pop star—just imagine someone announcing: "*Some Like It Hot,* starring Norma Jean Baker alias Marilyn Monroe"), and who, moreover, simply did not know enough about boxing, or, better, about the very different style of boxing that made Muhammad Ali so extraordinary and fascinating, and so with their babble contradicted precisely what had driven us to watch TV at that hour of the night—those people, then, don't need to be convinced by some long excursus on my part. We exchange glances, or so it seems, the way Rosicrucians or Freemasons do. But it has always been a little embarrassing to sit across from someone, be it man or woman, who could see in the whole business nothing more than Arno Schmidt's pronouncement about "prize-fighters who clubbed each other in the face while people gaped and paid."[1]

As is our wont, we go all intellectual and a bit sly. Didn't Alexander Sutherland Neill—yes, "Summerhill" Neill—write that he was always on the side of the underdog, even in boxing, with one exception: Muhammad Ali, whose boxing style he found "almost poetical"? Or Bertrand Russell, who surprised Ali with a transatlantic call to congratulate him on the position he had taken on Vietnam. Ali graciously reciprocated with an invitation for Russell to join him at ringside in London for the second Henry Cooper fight. Ali signed off on the call with an old standby phrase: "You're not as dumb as you look."[2]

In his autobiography Muhammad Ali tells that he learned only much later who it was he was speaking with and wrote a letter of apology. Russell didn't come to see the Ali vs. Cooper bout; nothing came of another planned meeting, either. And so, although they never met, Russell did follow up with a letter in which he expressed complete support for Ali's antiwar position and also warned him that those who held power in America would try to make his life miserable. "You have my wholehearted support," his letter concluded.[3]

Neill. Russell. Martin Luther King Jr. often sat in the first row at Muhammad Ali's fights. Malcolm X was seen at Ali's training camp—at a time when Muhammad Ali was still Cassius Clay. I once sat in a little dingy Indian restaurant in London, with paper tablecloths that had seen multiple use and all the rest on the seamier but ostensibly authentic side of things, and on the walls were nothing but wallpaper and a photograph of Muhammad Ali.

London, 1966. The bout to which Muhammad Ali had invited Bertrand Russell was one of his truly strange ones. It looked as if Ali wanted to prove to the grand old pacifist that you can win a prizefight without using your fists. It was the second Ali vs. Cooper bout. Their previous fight—18 June 1963—was one of three in which Ali, still Cassius Clay at the time, was sent to the canvas. The first occurred before his professional days and so need not interest us; the third was his first match with Joe Frazier; and when you compare the two, you notice that it was an almost identical punch in both cases, but never had Ali been, or would he ever again be, in such trouble as after Henry Cooper's left hook in 1963. Like Cooper's punch, Frazier's left hook sent him to the mat, but as if it was the sheer impact of the blow and not the brief state of unconsciousness that caused him to buckle and collapse, Ali was able to get up and—aware perhaps that he no longer had to fight to win the match and looking almost relaxed, with hands resting on the ropes and weight balanced nicely on his back leg—wait out the count. In London, Cassius Clay likewise managed to get to his feet, even though the punch had almost sent him tumbling through the ropes, but, as the cliché has it, he was saved by the bell. Clay's trainer, Angelo Dundee, claiming some sort of trouble with the gloves, extended the pause between rounds, and Clay shook off the effects of his brief blackout. In the next round the fight had to be interrupted because Clay's jabs had ripped

Cooper's eyebrow open. Head wounds are notorious for bleeding dramatically—biology's tribute to the intellect?—and for the good of both aesthetics and Cooper, who was blinded by his own blood, the fight was stopped.[4]

In the 1966 bout Muhammad Ali—as he is now named—at first attempts to avoid this unavoidably bloody side of his profession. That will not always be the case: "The Bleeder [Wepner] is duly bled," begins the chapter entitled "Looking Glass Country" in Wilfrid Sheed's *Muhammad Ali,* and Sheed is referring to the underdog boxer whom Ali managed to defeat only on points and who for a brief moment looked as if he would be the third man capable of decking Ali. The film of the fight reveals that he stepped on Ali's foot, causing him to stumble. Wepner was then used as the role model for one of Hollywood's most successful characters, "Rocky." But more of that later. "The Bleeder is duly bled. Chuck Wepner is dragged to his corner like a dead bull, after fifteen rounds of torture— mental and physical. Anyone who's forgotten that this is a bloody business Ali's engaged in is set straight by a quick glance at Wepner's punctured veins and the red stains on his trunks. A few feet away, David Anderson's typewriter is still caked with George Chuvalos's blood, courtesy of your favorite pacifist."[5]

Then 1966. In his rematch with Cooper, Ali doesn't punch much, or hard; and at first, when he does, in an amazingly unorthodox way for his style. Ali tries to keep his distance and land body blows at a slight diagonal from above. He makes no use of chances to land hard jabs to the head and spends the first round staying out of the way. The whole affair looks curious. The stronger man avoids punching; the other is untiring in his attempts to punch. That's the story from the first round to the fifth. For the most part, Ali dodges Cooper's attack. When that doesn't work, he goes into a clinch until the referee separates them. Sometimes he simply shoves Cooper—who is not just untiring but also increasingly angry—away. When he does make rare attempts to land a punch, it looks as if he wants to make clear to everyone watching just what would happen if he kept it up. In fact, he does just enough to keep from being disqualified for failing to fight. In case anyone is of the opinion, however, that you can win a boxing match by avoiding hitting your opponent with your fists, he's wrong. Between rounds five and six, it appears to have become clear to Ali that if this method of fighting has shown respect for his opponent's physical vulnerability, it shows none for the European champion's boxing skills. All the same, Ali holds back in round six, until the inevitable happens: a right jab opens Cooper's left eyebrow. Two, three more punches enlarge the wound. The referee checks the damage and lets the fight go on. Ali proceeds accordingly, Cooper finds himself in a hail of blows, Ali chases him around the ring, Cooper no longer even sees the punches coming, he reels back, blood flowing down his face in streams. The referee stops the fight.

"The aesthetic nerves quiver to regress into the Stone Age"[6] is one of Adorno's many malicious aphorisms on Stravinsky's *Le Sacre du Printemps*. In his

Felix Krull, Thomas Mann has Kuckuck, a paleontologist, say somewhat more amenably: "Progress exists, Kuckuck said, . . . exists beyond any doubt, from *Pithecanthropus erectus* to Newton and Shakespeare, it is a wide road leading most assuredly upward. But just as is the case with the rest of Nature, so, too, in the human world: here, too, everything is always congregated together, every state of culture and morals, everything, from the earliest to the latest, from the most stupid to the most clever, from the most primal, dull, and savage to what is most highly refined and developed, exists cheek by jowl in this world all at once, indeed often what is most refined grows wearied of itself, becomes infatuated with what is most primal and sinks drunkenly back into a state of savagery."[7] Is that really what this is? The permission to regress into a fantasized primal state, granted by our "favorite pacifist"—"Keep asking me, no matter how long/On the war in Viet Nam, I sing this song/I ain't got no quarrel with the Viet Cong."[8]

Intellectuals are constrained by their profession to have problems with expressing aggression. A victory on paper is one that can never be proved. Besides which, intellectuals are paid to delineate complexities. A boxing match is simple; and when someone is lying on the mat and doesn't get back on his feet after ten seconds, there are no hermeneutical problems, either. But then why don't we ("we" in the restricted sense noted above) love Mike Tyson, the master of every stark simplicity and a truly atavistic type; why not Sonny Liston, or the young George Foreman? Is it merely out of some vestige of shame that we admit our love, if love we must, only for the more subtly distinctive fighter? Or maybe it really isn't infatuation with "what is most primal," because one has grown "wearied" of oneself. After all, one would rather not forfeit the ability to write an essay on the subject that uses "wearied" and not just "weary." Does one, do "we," not want simply to be a little more all-embracing? Do we not perhaps want the certainty of knowing that we reach for the pen because we choose to refrain from pummeling each other with fists, and so rid ourselves of the foolish suspicion that we really have no other choice?

Which brings us back to the attraction of Jack London. He has a lot of readers, including intellectuals, even leftists, who will tell you that London was a "socialist." He may have seen it that way, but he was, of course, more like a left-wing Fascist. He is also the man who induced James Jeffries to come out of retirement to fight Jack Johnson, the first black world champion, and who coined the phrase "the great white hope": "Jim Jeffries must emerge from his alfalfa farm in California and remove the golden smile from Jack Johnson's face. Jeff, it's up to you."[9] Nevertheless, *Martin Eden* isn't a bad book, and *The Sea-Wolf* isn't, either— just to be explicitly intellectual. Interestingly enough, Fascism never had much luck with boxers. Mussolini would have made an excellent carny boxer, but the good Italian boxers were all Americans: Primo Carnera, Rocky Marciano, Rocky Graziano (and, of course, "Rocky"—Sylvester Stallone, "the Italian Stallion"). The

Nazis had Max Schmeling, and had no luck with him. He looked a lot like Jack Dempsey, but he became world champion in 1931 only because his opponent was disqualified for hitting below the belt. He lost the return match on points, but since the decision met with general disapproval, he became extremely popular. Hitler invited him to dinner.

Schmeling goes up against Max Baer in 1930. Max Baer is Jewish and wears a Star of David on his shorts, but the letter inside it isn't a "J" for "Jew," but an "M" for "Max." As best he can inside the ring, Baer obeys a call from ringside—"Kill that Nazi, Jewboy!" After ten rounds, Max Schmeling is no longer able to defend himself. Granted, three years later he defeated the young Joe Louis, earning him another invitation to dine with Hitler. He lost to Louis again shortly thereafter. Every German over forty grew up with the name "Max Schmeling," a fact that warrants a quick glance in our direction. Well into middle age, Schmeling remained a favorite with the Germans. He looked a lot like Dempsey, he boxed the way they imagined an Aryan should box, and he once knocked out Joe Louis in the twelfth round. What more could a German boxing fan want?

But if "Schmeling" sounds odd to American ears, what about "Muhammad Ali"? As "Cassius Clay," would Muhammad Ali have been something more than just a world champion boxer? Is that a foolish question simply because by changing his name he wanted to prove that he was something more? But what does "more" mean? What is a heavyweight champion "less than"? Maybe we all should change our names every ten years.

Incognito. No, *Outis*. It is also essential to the Enlightenment's dialectic that the "man of many ways" not only had to break Circe's spell in the sense of a Weberian demystification, but he also could not have laid claim to the throne had he not succeeded in hand-to-hand combat with a beggar. I gladly grant scholars of myth that participating in anything so vulgar with human scum may be a pre-Christian descent into hell, but if passing a test is proof of divinity, is brawling not also proof of princely bearing? ". . . and both men put their hands up./At that time, much-enduring great Odysseus pondered/whether to hit him so that the life would go out of him, as he/went down, or only to stretch him out by hitting him lightly./And in the division of his heart this way seemed best to him,/to hit him lightly, so the Achaians would not be suspicious./They put up their hands, and Iros hit him on the right shoulder,/but Odysseus struck the neck underneath the ear, and shattered/the bones within, and the red blood came in his mouth, filling it./He dropped, bleating, in the dust, with teeth set in a grimace,/and kicking at the ground with his feet. . . ."[10]

And this is what Wieland has his Aristippus of Cyrene say about the Olympic Games: "As noon wore on and the sun burned upon our pates, the cruel spectacle provided us by the cold-blooded rage of boxers and the dreadful gloves with which a few pairs of new Eryxes and Herculeses pulverized one another even filled me at first with a strange sort of terrible and tragic pleasure, in that it seemed to transport me to the old Heroic Age and make real to me the poets' tales of those most incredible deeds performed by the sons of the gods. I fancied I saw before me some kind of indestructible Titanic figures who merely played at setting upon one another so fiercely, and for whom the wounds they inflicted upon each other would no doubt close again as quickly and as scarless as the very air rent by their mighty blows. But that illusion was of brief duration; and when, after barely a quarter hour's struggle, I saw them carry from the lists one of the athletes, who moments before had presented the beauty of a Paris or Nireus united with the strength of a Milanion and who could have been the model for a statue of Apollo himself but was now so badly mangled that not a trace of his former lineaments was discernible in his battered face or indeed on his entire body now pounded to an unshapely mass, that ghastly sight so o'erwhelmed me that I could not restrain myself from giving vent to my horror with a loud cry, which luckily was heard by no one . . . amid the tumult and jubilation of the spectators."[11]

There's really no talking your way around that. Progress, if it exists, leads away from a punch in the face. If a reader, whether female or male, should nevertheless choose to follow me, I must point out to her or him that one does not praise a writer by saying he was a good cross-country runner, or a boxer by saying he was not just a boxer. Only someone who achieves something in his profession should let himself be praised for being talented in other ways as well. Only because Muhammad Ali was a great boxer was he some other things, too. He was "more than a champion" because he was the best and most interesting *boxer* there had ever been until then. People did not watch his boxing matches because they were something other than boxing matches, but because as *these* boxing matches they were something different from all other boxing matches. Do you follow me?

MANILA, I–III

Q uezon City near Manila, 1 October 1975; Muhammad Ali vs. Joe Frazier. Bell for the first
round. A few steps bring the two boxers to the center of
the ring. Muhammad Ali holds both fists almost level
with his eyes; below his shoulders the body is turned
a little to the right of its vertical axis, the left leg
advanced and slightly bent at the knee, the right
stretched backward, the way a fencer would hold his
body for a lunge. Both fists, however, are approximately the same distance from his opponent. This is
Ali's way of offering the smallest possible area to body

blows from Joe Frazier, the smaller man, while at the same time retaining for himself the possibility of attacking with either his left or his right. Frazier stands bent forward, holding his gloves at chest level, tapping them together as if eager to go to work. Ali will attack with jabs, will try to hit Frazier's head and make the most of his longer reach. Frazier will try to dodge under the jabs and either hit Ali low in the ribs or land a left or right hook higher up. It is the third time that Ali and Frazier have faced each other in the ring.

Not only does Ali have to win this fight, he has to win it convincingly, whatever that means. In 1971, he lost their first bout—promoted like five to seven others as "the Battle of the Century"—and with that loss, three and a half years after his boxing license had been revoked for his refusal to serve in the army, his attempt to regain the title foundered. Before the rematch in 1974, Ali fought thirteen times, twice against Ken Norton, who won their first bout (Norton broke Ali's jaw in the second round) and lost the second by only a few points. When Ali and Frazier met again, Frazier was no longer world champion. George Foreman had knocked him down six times in just two rounds—after which the referee ended the fight. Ali's decisive victory on points had evened the score, so to speak, but that was all. That fight had more or less been a private affair between two ex–world champions. That Ali had been undefeated as world champion hardly counted after his failed attempt to defeat the current champion, and meant nothing, then, when he failed to defeat Frazier as convincingly as the new world champion, George Foreman, had done. No wonder, then, that when Ali and Foreman met in Kinshasa in 1974, Foreman was the favorite, and Ali's victory by a knockout in the eighth round turned out to be one of the most sensational ever in the history of professional boxing. If Ali were to lose in Manila, not only would he lose his title, but the win in Kinshasa would also perhaps be called into question as merely a stroke of luck, and the same would hold true in case of a narrow victory. Any win that did not stand out as something special would mean only that the score was now two to one for Ali, nothing more. "Looking back, people say that Ali–Frazier III was a great fight. And it was; one of the greatest of all time. But going in, a lot of people didn't even think it would be a good fight. Frazier had been turned into a yo-yo by George Foreman. Ali had not looked good after Zaire. . . ."[12]

After the bell ending round one, on his way back to his corner Frazier taps Ali on the knee. Whatever that may mean, it is at any rate not a gesture of respect. It has been a fast first round; Ali hit Frazier with left and right jabs, but Frazier also landed a couple of punches, one of them his feared left hook (it was a left hook that, as noted, had sent Ali to the canvas in 1971), and for a moment Ali took cover behind his raised fists and leaned against the ropes. But almost at once he pounds Frazier with several hard combinations. Frazier, to be sure, had been the winner of "the Battle of the Century," but he had taken enough punches to the head that he spent a few days resting in the hospital under observation.

Ali's big wins were all against boxers considered "unbeatable"—Sonny Liston, George Foreman. With intelligence and elegance Ali outmaneuvered them. What became clear, could not help becoming clear in the match with Foreman—because Ali didn't dance light-footedly around his opponent, keeping up a flurry of punches from a distance, as he had in his first bout with Liston, but instead spent a large part of the fight almost stationary, leaning against the ropes—was Ali's amazing capacity to "take it," as boxing jargon puts it. Ali could shake off punches (had been able to do so early on, but because of his other qualities people hadn't noticed) that would have dropped other men, and he could endure pain that would have robbed them of their courage. All this, however, would first be clear to everyone in Manila.

In Manila, however, Ali was not facing a Liston or a Foreman, or even a Mike Tyson—whom it took only a certain James ("Buster") Douglas to finish off as a boxer. Frazier was strong, stronger than Ali, who was widely regarded not to be one of the "big punchers" (but rather to be a "stylist," even though fourteen of his twenty-two world championship bouts did not go the distance, and were won by KOs, by his opponent throwing in the towel, or by the referee stopping the fight), but Frazier was not a man who relied on landing a decisive blow, the way Liston and Foreman had, who then didn't understand the world when by the third round they hadn't yet succeeded in decking their opponent. That meant Ali could not count on simply surviving the first few rounds, leaving him to face a frustrated, emotionally fatigued opponent. Frazier could go the full fifteen and at the final bell still pack a left hook with unflagging enthusiasm—and with that same hook he had once succeeded in knocking the pins out from under Ali. Frazier's strategy was clear, as were his tactics, since they both came down to the same thing: to land blows that, as he said later, would have "knocked a building over"; to trust that the older Ali would not go the distance, would tire, with pain too great for him to look elegant or confident; and so in that way to score his decisive points in the last few rounds (the first rounds would go to Ali in any case). And there was always the possibility of a lethal punch like the one in 1971. The possibility, although Frazier wasn't relying on it, but on a long, wearying fight full of pain.

Ali, on the other hand, had to get used to the idea that he would not be able to put the stamp of his own style on the fight, as he had so often succeeded in doing, especially with Liston and Foreman. The main thing for Ali was not to be sent to the canvas and to still have enough strength by the end of the fight to "look good." The only way to cut this frustrating business short was to hit Frazier so often and hard at the start— not with one "decisive" punch but dozens of times, till his opponent's senses were frayed and confused—that a lightning-fast combination of three, four, five jabs would end in a KO. That's how Ali had won against Oscar Bonavena, an Argentinean boxer who had looked as if you could not have got past him with a sledge-hammer, and against whom Ali did not cut an especially good figure for fourteen rounds, until in the fifteenth he knocked him down three times. Except— Frazier was no Bonavena, and he knew Ali. Ali knew Frazier, too, of course, but the fact that Ali knew how Frazier would fight gave him no advantage, which was not the case with Frazier's knowledge of Ali's style. Ali was always dominant, brilliant, whenever he could surprise, and thus his victories over Liston and Foreman are among the great artistic masterpieces of boxing history. But that was precisely what Frazier did not permit Ali to be: surprising. He forced his own style on Ali, keeping him "below par," so to speak. Ali could display his repertoire as much as he liked; he could dance on light feet around Frazier, hitting his face with a flurry of quick left jabs; he could move to the ropes and let Frazier punch away in hopes that he would batter himself tired against Ali's defense; he could deliver a hard combination to Frazier that would have sent other men to their knees—in the end Frazier just kept marching forward, striking untiringly with his heavy right and left hooks. That was the reason the experts did not even expect a good fight. The first two Ali–Frazier bouts had indeed supplied everything a boxing fan enjoys: energy, courage, stamina, technical perfection (but no knockout); but for those who loved Muhammad Ali's fights they were less gratifying. Not only because you always want your own favorite to win, but because they showed hardly any of what was called "Ali's magic," and had little to do with what probably awaited you in Manila: pain and heroism.

Looking back on the fight, Frazier's trainer Eddie Futch said that he had not expected the first round to be so fast and hard. "A great round for Muhammad Ali," says the commentator, adding that Frazier usually loses the first few rounds. He is expecting the fight to run a normal course: first Ali will score points, then Frazier, and the winner will be whoever totals the most. But the second round shows a dominating Ali, a man who wants more than just to increase his points on the judges' cards. He sovereignly, almost ironically, dodges one of Frazier's hulking hooks, keeps his arm outstretched, holding his smaller opponent at a distance, and suddenly strikes without giving Frazier so much as a chance to cover himself. Frazier does manage to get in a few punches that send Ali retreating to the ropes, but the answer is always a hard jab to the head. Another brief moment now, in which Ali leans against the ropes covering his face with both gloves, his forearms protecting his upper body clear down to the solar plexus. It looks as if Ali wants to quote from his earlier fights—the same defense he used against George Foreman, which he called "rope-a-dope," leading with his left the way he did in the fifth round of his first match with Liston. There is no doubt Ali is the superior boxer. But how much weight should you give to the impression of two rounds? Frazier ends the second, after the bell, with a disparaging wave of his left hand: That's all you've got? He's learned this from Ali, who replied to Foreman's most terrible blows with taunting remarks, giving himself time to shake off his partial befuddlement. Worse than the gesture is Frazier's smile, which he never loses, even when he's hit.

Frazier comes out of his corner smiling, taps his gloves together, and resolutely lays into Ali. The round begins with a furious, almost "open" exchange of punches. Then Ali retreats to the ropes. Frazier strikes, and lands the punch despite Ali's double guard. "Rope-a-dope" makes less sense against Frazier's method of attack than it did against Foreman, and besides, even when he only hits Ali's guard, Frazier doesn't strike "glancing blows" but hits as if he wants to knock over that building. Foreman had worn himself out on Ali's guard because he believed he'd win in a few rounds; Foreman wanted to "land one." Frazier is counting on fifteen rounds from the start, but at some point, in the twelfth or thirteenth, Ali's arms are going to hurt so bad that using them to cover will hurt worse than the punch they're supposed to ward off. Frazier's blows to Ali's arms are not wasted, and Frazier knows it. That's why he's smiling. But Frazier doesn't wear himself out. He hits precisely—striking the body now to the left, now to the right of Ali's cover, then higher between the arms; usually the hook doesn't connect, but not always. Ali shoves Frazier back, then waves his fist: Okay, go ahead and punch! That doesn't look right—it, too, is a quotation, but it seems hackneyed. Then Frazier connects with a left hook. The reply is a hail of blows from Ali, a series of hard jolts. But Frazier connects again; and again. Now it's Frazier who's on the ropes, but only briefly. An exchange of punches in the center of the ring, then Frazier drives Ali to the corner. Bell.

BIOGRAPHY

Cassius Marcellus Clay, later Muhammad Ali, was born in Louisville, Kentucky, on 17 January 1942, the son of a sign painter with artistic ambitions. He begins to box early, at age twelve; at eighteen he wins an Olympic gold medal as a light heavyweight. He signs a contract with eleven Louisville businessmen who guarantee him both a steady income and an old-age pension (and for athletes, boxers in particular, a pension starts to be an interesting topic when they're just in their early thirties). All in all, he appears to have been in fairly good hands, although this Louisville

Sponsoring Group does not come off especially well in Ali's autobiography or in the infinitely dreadful (and, what is really quite a trick, boring) film based on it. If it is true that the contract stipulated that the group would receive 50 percent of all of Clay's income, it would have had to be renegotiated at the latest after he won the world championship. But it never comes to that. When he becomes champion by defeating Sonny Liston, Ali leaves his sponsors, converts to Islam, and abandons the name Clay.

But, as noted, first an Olympic victory. As he tells it in his "own story," he threw the gold medal in the Ohio when he couldn't get served in a restaurant because of his skin color. Whether the story is true or not, it is possible. It's also possible that when Clay brought out his medal to prove he wasn't just anybody, the restaurant owner said both "I don't give a damn *who* he is!" and "We don't serve no niggers!" It may also be that it's a nice invention by Durham, his autobiographer, because in retrospect the schadenfreude was just too great— serves you right, rednecks.

Sixteen bouts go by after the Olympic win before we run across an opponent's name that means anything to us (presuming that names of boxers mean anything at all to us): Archie Moore. Archie Moore had once held the world light-heavyweight title and was forty-eight at the time of their bout. The interesting thing is that Moore had briefly worked as Clay's trainer. Clay had dumped Moore because Moore wouldn't accept Clay's boxing style and wanted to teach Clay how to box correctly. Clay was quite right not to want to be taught *that,* and someone found Angelo Dundee instead, who will always remain one of the truly great trainers, not least because he knew how to make the best of the idiosyncrasies of the men he was training. Moore, in any case, came into the fight with the explicit wish to thrash his disobedient pupil, and how badly mistaken about Clay he had been as a trainer was apparent from the fact that he even thought his wish possible. Clay prophesied a KO based on rhyme: "Moore in four," and fulfilled the prophecy by holding back in the early rounds.

It was at about this time that Clay began to get on the press's nerves by predicting what round he would win in, and the prophecies would get printed along with comments about what an insufferable loudmouth Clay was—which, then, was ultimately the point. Clay was the man who really understood that sports are a branch of entertainment, and so resorted to appropriate methods. That he would later break his own rules— or again, maybe not—by giving his athletic career the quality of a political crusade, yet always with a tinge of irony, makes him, perhaps, the first postmodern strategist. But that strategy could never have worked, of course, if he had not (almost) always run up against a concentrated eagerness to find him annoying. There is a film of an interview in which a white reporter can only barely contain himself, as if he were—yes, what?—Ali's boss, teacher, the man in charge of someone he's been paid a flat fee, or maybe by the hour, to question, and he jumps on Clay, asking if he can't keep his mouth shut for once. A peculiar question for someone conducting an interview. Clay replies with such an open and totally unnaïve smile: "You know, that's impossible." And he turns away from the indignant interviewer to look directly into the camera, although the shot is set up to get the two of them in profile. And that look says both You won't shut me up and How absurd to make a question like this the topic for an interview. As for his prophecies, he says: Everyone wants to break records, Kennedy predicted an American would walk on the moon before 1970, and so I predict I'll be the next heavyweight champ. And he says something else that is indeed very strange: "I'm going to break Floyd Patterson's record." Now, Floyd Patterson set only one record, by breaking the classic law of professional boxing: They never come back. After losing the championship in 1959 to Ingemar Johansson, Patterson won it back in their rematch. Muhammad Ali was in fact the first man to win the world championship three times. And yet for someone who was not even champ yet, this look ahead to the, shall we say, difficulties of his later years is quite remarkable.

As he predicts, he will end the fight with Henry Cooper, the future European champ, in five rounds, even though he already sends him to the mat in the fourth. The next bout is with Sonny Liston, for the world championship. Judging by the bets taken on the fight, Cassius Clay is the clear underdog—the bookies' odds on Liston are 8 to 1. Who in his right mind would want to fight this bear of a man? Everyone said that he was as mean as he was big—and they may very well have been right. He had spent five years in prison for armed robbery, and had learned to box there. Liston grew up fighting in alleys without any Marquis of Queensberry rules. He may have got used to them in prison bouts, but by instinct he was a street brawler. After a few successful fights, Liston beats up a policeman who tries to give a ticket to the driver of a taxi Liston is riding in. The policeman lands in the hospital, Liston back in jail. Released again, he is soon regarded as the real world heavyweight champion; the man who holds the title, Floyd Patterson, tries to avoid a fight for a while. It takes place on 25 September 1962, and Liston wins by a KO after two minutes and six seconds.

Liston becomes an almost mythical figure. People say he's unbeatable; they not only compare him with Jack Johnson, Jack Dempsey, and Rocky Marciano, but rank him higher, and even believe he could have beaten Joe Louis at the top of his form. You can't say more about a boxer than that. Sportswriters were quick to proclaim that Sonny Liston was the strongest heavyweight fighter ever to climb into the ring. He could punch harder than anybody, they said, and he could also take the hardest punches anybody had to dish out. He was granite. And so forth. And if no one today counts Liston among the great world champions (after he won against them, most of Ali's opponents were said to have been overrated), we still should keep in mind his status at the time. The press in fact considered him the best and most dangerous heavyweight ever—his reputation was at least as devastating as Mike Tyson's at the peak of his career. When you look at the

Liston–Patterson fight, you can begin to understand why. Floyd Patterson doesn't even get around to establishing his style; even his defense against Liston amounts to nothing more than clinches. After six or eight heavy blows, Patterson falls down.

In the second Liston–Patterson fight, Liston takes four seconds longer to knock Patterson out. In the rematch, Liston was the 5-to-1 favorite—so you can see how much the experts, the reporters, and the prospective audience for a Liston–Clay fight, thought of the latter. Clay used the fight against Patterson to announce his own claim to a title fight. The fight was held in Las Vegas, where Sonny had Floyd Patterson to deal with inside the ring. But outside the ropes was an even bigger problem, a fighter named Cassius Clay who kept shooting off his mouth. Clay had constructed a public relations campaign unlike any before it. The goal was first, as someone who seemed to have no chance in the ring, just to get a fight, and second, to attract as much attention to it as possible in order to increase the purse. In pursuing this campaign, Clay intentionally violated some of the rules of deportment that athletes, especially black boxers, are supposed to follow—most especially, the one that said "Be modest." Liston would fall in eight, Clay prophesied, usually adding some disparaging remark about Liston, who was ugly and slow. The main slogan of the campaign was "I am The Greatest!" and the public picked up on the term, at first reluctantly and then over the years with growing respect. In the beginning, however, this black "loudmouth" was a scandal—hadn't Clay said that he was not just The Greatest but the most beautiful, too? It's true Clay was good-looking, and not just "for a boxer." It is also true that in a boxer beauty is a surprising attribute—anyone who places any value on not just having but also keeping a handsome face shouldn't box. But the real scandal, of course, lay elsewhere. It was a black man who talked about himself that way—and at a time when the phrase "Black is beautiful" had not yet been coined, at a time when chemicals for lightening black skin were sold in drugstores. For enhancing self-perception and increasing self-confidence, Clay/Ali perhaps did more than Martin Luther King Jr., Malcolm X, Patrice Lumumba, and Bill Cosby combined—and not just in America.

For whites, Clay's shameless (in the best sense) behavior reawakened unpleasant memories of Jack Johnson, the world champion from 1908 to 1915. Johnson had been the first black man to become world champion, and his equally shameless self-assurance had earned him naked hatred. Johnson was indeed the first propagandist for "Black is beautiful," but in fact, just as with the young Cassius Clay, all he had said, paraphrasing Ariosto, was that he himself was beautiful: "After God made me, he broke the mold." Unlike the later Cassius Clay turned Muhammad Ali, Johnson was a totally apolitical man, but his victories led to racial unrest, and the film of his defeat of "the great white hope," the ex-champ Jim Jeffries—who wanted and was expected (as the propagandistic Jack London had written) to win back the title—was banned from being shown in public.

One would have a difficult time keeping separate what was Ali's own self-confidence and what was behavioral therapy, what was political conviction and what was pure PR. "I began predicting the outcome of my fights," Clay once explained, "after watching Gorgeous George, the great wrestler. I heard this white fellow say, 'I am the World's Greatest Wrestler! I cannot be defeated. I am The Greatest! I am the King. If that sucker mess up the pretty waves in my hair, I'm gonna kill him. If that sucker whups me, I'm gonna get the next jet to Russia. I cannot be defeated. I am the prettiest. I am the greatest!' And when he was in the ring, everybody booooooed, booooooed. Oh, everybody just booed. And I was mad. And I looked around and saw everybody was mad. . . . I saw 15,000 people coming to see this man get beat. And his talking did it. And, I said, this is a g-o-o-o-o-o-o-o-d idea!"[13] And in fact Clay filled arenas with people who wanted to see just one thing: a defeated, humbled Clay. Ali later recalled one woman in particular, who went by the name of Miss Velvet Green and made a point of telling him that she was at ringside for all his fights, because, she said, "God won't always let evil win! . . . I'm going to be there when they bust your face and stomp it in. . . . If there is a God . . . it's going to happen, and I want to be there."[14]

Clay rides around in a bus with slogans painted on it—another borrowed idea, this one from Budd Schulberg's *The Harder They Fall*. He drives past Liston's house at night and makes so much noise that Liston threatens to call the police. He has his photograph taken holding a rope and a sign that reads "Bear Hunt-ing." He does just about everything to call attention to himself, attention and dislike. Hardly anyone takes him seriously as a boxer. "Forty-three of the forty-six sports-writers in this country predicted that they couldn't see Clay walking out of the ring. Of course, many people saw in a Clay–Liston fight a chance for Clay's mouth to be finally closed. . . . Clay was aware of this and kept shooting off his mouth. The bragging forced Sonny to talk. 'If they ever make the fight,' Liston said, 'I'll be locked up for murder.'"[15]

An agreement for a fight is arranged—then Clay backs off. The purse isn't big enough. "I had talked too much and worked too hard to take a low financial cut, since I built it up, I'll tear it down. There will be no fight between Liston and I until the money is right. I'm the talk of the world. I am known as the predictor. 'The Big Bear' needs me. So if I have to take low, I had just rather not fight."[16] A couple of months later, a contract is signed. After that Clay sets in motion his propaganda campaign against Liston, whom he calls old and worn-out and, over and over, ugly. He prophesies a knockout in round eight, and adopts a slogan for his boxing style: "Float like a butterfly, sting like a bee."

Custom dictates that the two opponents meet briefly before the fight at the weigh-in. Clay uses this meeting, to which interested reporters are normally invited, to stage a final scene. He jumps around, shouting his "Float like a butterfly, sting like a bee!" and generally behaving so outrageously that when Liston enters the room he is greeted with "thunderous applause." Clay acts as if he wants to attack Liston on the spot. He can be held back only with difficulty, or so it would appear—the physician checks his pulse: 120 beats a second. Clay does not in fact seem to be entirely in control of himself. Was it simply fright, was he trying to cover up his fear? "Clay's voice grew more shrill. He moved his hands vigorously; he jumped and screamed and his eyes bugged. His body appeared to be shaken. It was startling. It was frightening. But it was an act. There was physical effort involved and probably some fear involved. Yet if Clay was afraid, it was a controlled fear, an energy Clay was accustomed to waste at pre-fight shows."[17] As Clay left the weigh-in room, he was calm, his pulse beating at a rate of 54 times a second, the normal rate for him. Liston did not know what to make of it all. Presumably he figured Clay was certifiably crazy.

The fight was a sensation, and a huge surprise, even to people who had not overrated Liston and had given Clay some chance, if not an especially large one. Liston does not respond to the bell for the seventh round. Frustrated and angry, his face badly battered, he sits in his corner. He has not had Clay in trouble even once, not even in the fifth round, when Clay had to fight almost blind because something had got in his eye. Clay, on the other hand, had been striking at will, and harder from round to round. Liston must have torn a muscle in his right arm with one of his many punches at empty air. His face showed equal anger and resignation as he threw in the towel.

I will discuss this fight in more detail later, because

there have been things written about it that simply are not true. For the fight revealed more than just the light-footed Clay who was always just beyond reach and kept Sonny Liston covered with a flurry of light left jabs. But we'll leave it at that for now. A press conference followed the fight, and the new world champion had every right to it: "I shook the world! I really must be The Greatest!" he shouted with that surplus of amazement that characterizes our happiness when wish and reality come together. When you look at this same boxer who's now over fifty, with his trembling hands and difficulty speaking, you see before you a man ruined by a few fights too many and by medical advice that was at best dilettantish—but, taken all in all, ruined by boxing itself. Yet in no other profession could Ali have achieved the heights from which he would one day have to fall. I assume few men have ever experienced such moments of triumph in their lives as Clay experienced when Liston refused to continue the fight. The question of what price anything is worth first gets asked when the price is to be paid, and if the day of reckoning occurs far beyond the day when the account was opened, the price almost always seems too high. But the question that lies behind it all is not one that deserves a facile answer.

At the press conference following the fight, Ali made sure he evened the score with the reporters. Before they could bombard him with questions, he had something to say himself: "'Hold it! Hold it!' I say. 'You've all had a chance to say what you thought before the fight. Now it's my turn. You all said Sonny Liston would kill me. You said he was better than Jack Johnson or Jack Dempsey, even Joe Louis, and you ranked them the best heavyweights of all time. You kept writing how Liston whipped Floyd Patterson twice, and when I told you I would get Liston in eight, you wouldn't believe it. Now I want all of you to tell the whole world while all the cameras are on us, tell the world that I'm The Greatest.' There's a silence. 'Who's The Greatest?' I ask them. Nobody answers. . . . 'For the LAST TIME! . . . WHO IS THE GREATEST?' They hesitate for a minute, and finally . . . they all answer, 'You are.'"[18]

There is a rematch. Depending on which version you accept, it lasts a minute and twenty seconds or two minutes and twelve seconds. Clay sends Liston to the mat with a left hook, the referee begins the count too late, and while he is debating with the other judges, Liston gets to his feet, the fight continues, and is finally stopped. No one, however, had seen the punch that knocked Liston down—was the fight, including the whole strange affair with the incompetent referee, fixed? Of course that was nonsense, since Clay had no lobby behind him that could have organized a fix like that—on the contrary. And to anyone looking at a tape of the fight it is clear that although Liston has his back half turned to the camera and Clay's right hand cannot be seen landing it, the punch was, as they say, "right on the button." Besides which, shortly after the fight Liston admitted to José Torres, the former light-heavyweight champ, that he had been hit.[19] Nevertheless, the phrase "phantom-punch" stuck.

Anyone who wants to know the truth about the two fights with Liston needs only to look at a photograph taken during the first fight. It can be found in Hauser's biography of Muhammad Ali (and elsewhere). Ali has just thrown a left jab, and it's clear that he is about to follow with his right. Liston is obviously expecting it, but not doing anything about it. His face shows not just pain—his brow is furrowed with worry like an old man's, the mouth is wrenched as if he is on the verge of crying. This mixture of helplessness, worry, and weeping combine to form an expression of fear—the fear that what has made him look like this can go on and on. Every hope for, or, better, every claim to, maintaining the title has been erased.

The first man to challenge the new world champion after Liston's second defeat is, ironically enough, Floyd Patterson. Patterson, José Torres writes, was the first black "white hope" in the history of boxing; he had announced that he wanted to "bring the championship back to America."[20] The fight was already politics. In *Soul on Ice,* Eldridge Cleaver saw it as follows: "The simplistic version of the fight bandied about in the press was that there was a 'white hope' and a 'black hope' riding on this fight. The white hope for a Patterson victory was, in essence, a counterrevolutionary desire to force the Negro, now in rebellion and personified in the boxing world by Ali, back into his 'place.' The black hope, on the contrary, was to see Lazarus crushed, to see Uncle Tom defeated, to be given symbolic proof of the victory of the autonomous Negro over the subordinate Negro."[21] The fight is stopped in the twelfth round, and many people suggested that Ali let it go on that long out of pure sadism, because Patterson had not only been completely outboxed, but he had also entered the match with a bad back. Torres, who is the author of the best and most carefully differentiated analyses of Ali's fights, thought that Patterson's total concentration on basic defense prevented the kind of surprise punch necessary for a knockout— at least when the man throwing it was not a "big puncher." Seven years later Ali managed a KO in the seventh round.

Even before the first fight with Liston, rumors were circulating that not only the Beatles had been seen in Clay's training camp, but Malcolm X as well, which seriously threatened to delay the fight, and Clay had promised to hold his peace until after the fight. Now he spoke again, loudly, and not just slogans about himself. He followed the example of Malcolm X and laid aside his "slave name"—almost every American black is the descendant of a slave, and liberated slaves often took the family names of their former owners, as a kind of "primal challenge." In addition to which, Clay converted to Islam, and not just that, he also joined the Nation of Islam (the "Black Muslims"), a sect that was led by the preacher Elijah Muhammad and to which Malcolm X also belonged. He did not call himself Cassius X, however (with the exception of one moment during his first induction into the American military), but rather was given the name Muhammad Ali by Elijah Muhammad. Between the first and second Liston fights, Malcolm X was shot and killed—under what circumstances it is still not clear even today, although at present it seems that people tend to believe the variation according to which Malcolm X was assassinated by the Nation of Islam because he had begun to turn away from it and its propaganda of strict apartheid. But then, perhaps it was the Ku Klux Klan—who knows?

Muhammad Ali not only behaved like a second Jack Johnson but also acted politically, was political, and had a political effect, and irritatingly, annoyingly, or provocatively declared himself to be a member of a group that not only could lay claim to a fair amount of obscurantism[22] but also definitely exceeded the civil rights movement in radicalness. Muhammad Ali termed the idea of racial integration "subjugation." He accepted the rhetoric of Malcolm X, who called black integrationists "Uncle Toms" and in one speech drew a clear distinction between "house" and "field" Negroes. If the slave owner's house caught fire, the "house Negro" would run inside and save his master's child; the "field Negro," however, would haul over bales of cotton to feed the flames. Ali makes it very obvious that he feels connected to the tradition of the "field Negro"—or let us put it this way: he made it easy for everyone to infer as much. Moreover, it became known before the fight with Patterson that Patterson, who lived in a "white" section of New York, had felt forced to sell his house because his neighbor's children called his kids "niggers." "I ain't never read anything more pitiful than how Patterson told the newspapers: 'I tried to integrate . . . it just didn't work.' . . . It is like when he was the champion. The only time he would be caught in Harlem was when he was in the back of a car waving in some parade. The big shot didn't have no time for his own kind, he was so busy integrating. And now he wants to fight me because I stick up for black people."[23] Moreover, Patterson had become a Catholic, that is, a member of a religion that, while not particularly exotic, is, for historical reasons, not all that widespread in the U.S., but nonetheless a Christian religion, a world religion; and since to this day the U.S. remains a nation dominated by Christianity, the whole affair became a struggle between two world religions in a country whose sympathies in the matter were quite unequivocal, even if no one had any idea of the problems Christian and, above all, Islamic fundamentalism would one day present to the world.

Added to all this, Muhammad Ali refused to serve in the army. The first time he was inducted, he failed to pass muster because he was unable to solve certain problems on the intelligence test. Later, when the war needed more soldiers, the draft board lowered its standards, and Cassius Clay was found fit for war. Ali got the news from television reporters and reacted as if it were a bothersome annoyance—what was the point, after all, he didn't have no quarrel with the Viet Cong. That statement was not only unpatriotic, but to every patriot, from rednecks to Miss Velvet Green, it was snotnosed and uppity. First, an inductee's own concerns are not what is of importance, but rather the concerns of his native land, which render all other concerns unimportant; and second, the struggle against Communism in Southeast Asia was not something somebody could simply designate as a "quarrel." One can assume that the decision to draft Ali was not totally uninfluenced by public opinion. Torres supplies a few letters to the selective service, one of which, for example, reads: "When are you going to have the guts to bring that lousy, loudmouthed, un-American, cowardly, nigger back home and put him in the Army where we all hope he'll have his head shot off!"[24]

In the meantime, Ali had accepted a fight with the challenger, Ernie Terrell,[25] but Terrell had some sort of connection to the "underworld," which is always latently present in professional boxing (and one dare not forget that Ali's own connection with the Black Muslims, who had no problems with the use of force, guaranteed him protection in this regard), and this prevented the fight from being staged in New York; everyone then agreed on Chicago. But the state of Illinois can refuse to license any boxer who is not of "good and stable moral character" or commits acts "detrimental to the honesty of boxing," and by that they did not mean Terrell's connection to some sort of criminal syndicate, but Ali's statement "Ain't got no quarrel with the Viet Cong." The matter would have to go before the Illinois boxing commission; the governor got involved, calling Ali's remarks "disgusting," and Chicago's Mayor Daley asked the boxing commissioners to ban the fight.

A hearing was called, but the commission could not reach a decision. Ali apologized for his statement—not for its contents, but for having made it to the press and not the draft board. If his statements had caused anyone financial difficulties, he was ready to apologize for that. But in reply to the question whether he would apologize for his "unpatriotic remarks," he flat out refused. The fight could not take place in Illinois—the commission decided 2 to 1 against Ali. Ali's hometown of Louisville declined to serve as the site; other cities followed. The fight couldn't be staged in the U.S., and so they tried Canada. Terrell refused to fight there. His strategy was clear: he was speculating that as a result of his troubles with the authorities, Ali would be drafted or end up in prison, and in that case Terrell had a better chance of winning the requisite number of elimination bouts to become undisputed champion.

Ali accepted a fight with the Canadian George Chuvalo instead. It had been a long time since a world champion had fought for so little money,[26] and it ended in a victory on points after fifteen rounds. This was followed by a rematch with the Englishman Henry Cooper, and Ali remained in England to take on Brian London, whom he defeated in three rounds. The foreign tour continued on to Germany, where the Ali–Mildenberger fight was decided in twelve rounds.

Meanwhile there was the wait for Ali to be drafted into the U.S. Army and sent for duty in Vietnam. The uproar over Ali's unpatriotic remarks had apparently died down a little, so that fights had again become possible in the U.S.—against Cleveland Williams, Ernie Terrell, Zora Folley. After those bouts, no one any longer doubted Ali's right to hold the title.[27] He had proved that he could force his style on any boxer, that he could reply to the challenge of any other style, that he was faster and more precise than his opponents

but could also punch as hard and effectively as they—
and take more punches himself. And apart from all that,
Muhammad Ali's fights—always presuming that a person has any use at all for prizefights—were full of excitement and elegance. They were, if it is permissible to
say so about something as crude as a brawl, more intel-
ligent than anything anyone had ever seen before in
the boxing ring.

Then Ali was inducted, and as a conscientious objector refused to serve in the military. He based his claim
on the fact that he was a minister in the Nation of Islam
and on the right of free exercise of religion as guaranteed by the American Constitution. With that, his
world champion title was revoked, and for over three
years he could not obtain a license to box in any state.
Muhammad Ali was at the peak of his career; he was in
his mid-twenties—a boxer's finest years. Liston had
won the title at age thirty and lost it at thirty-three; Patterson held it from twenty-two to twenty-eight; Joe
Louis became world champion at twenty-two and held
on to the title until he was thirty-six; Rocky Marciano
won the title when he was twenty-nine and retired at
thirty-two; Jack Dempsey, from twenty-four to thirty-
two. When Ali was allowed to fight again after this
enforced pause, he was twenty-eight—not yet quite
past his best years. But in the first place, he had not
been in the ring for three years, and second, his special
talents were those typical of a young boxer: speed and
agility. As a boxer "ages"—that is, from his mid-twenties
on—he gets slower, but stronger, too; what he loses in
speed he gains in body weight and power in his fists.

That pays off for a "puncher," who gains from what he has always depended on and gives up what was never his forte, but not for a "stylist," who grows unsure whether he can compensate for his losses. The reporters were all in agreement after those first fights: Ali didn't have it anymore. "He's not the dancer we expected," read one typical comment. "This is a flat-footed Ali." They all yearn to have "the old Ali," "the young Cassius Clay," back.

Ali obtains his first boxing license in the South, of all places. He fights Jerry Quarry and wins in the third round. Then he defeats the Argentinean Oscar Bonavena by a knockout in the fifteenth. The next fight was the first against Joe Frazier. During the period when Ali could not get a boxing license, Frazier had won several elimination bouts and had been declared world champion, and now it had to be decided if he was champ beyond any doubt. Ali lost on points; the final round saw him floored by a left hook. Ali was the winner of the rematch—only on points, but the clear winner. But something had happened between those two fights. Ali had won on points or by a knockout against Jimmy Ellis, Buster Mathis, Jürgen Blin, and Mac Foster, against George Chuvalo, Jerry Quarry (again), and Al Lewis, against, curiously enough, Floyd Patterson (again), Bob Foster, and Joe Bugner, who had succeeded Henry Cooper as European champ. Then he went up against Ken Norton, who, besides being a professional boxer, had costarred in the notorious film *Mandingo* and was the first modern bodybuilder type in the ring. Norton broke Ali's jaw, presumably in the second round, and Ali lost on points. In a rematch with Norton, he won on points, but not "convincingly." Then followed a disappointing victory on points against Rudi Lubbers in Djakarta.

It is not without significance that Ali and his autobiographer have their book, *The Greatest: My Own Story*, begin with the defeat by Ken Norton: "Louisville 100 miles. I barely see the sign in the rain. . . . Until now, I had always come home like the victorious hunter bringing back big game from the jungle: two Golden Gloves Championships, some AAU titles, an Olympic Gold Medal, the World Heavyweight Title. Even exiled and barred from boxing, I came back as The Undefeated.

"Now it's the spring of 1973 and I'm coming home after a defeat every man, woman and child in my hometown saw or heard about, just like everybody else all over the world."[28]

Ali had then fought against Joe Frazier a second time, and won. But Frazier was no longer world champion; he had been decked several times in his first two rounds against George Foreman, so that the referee had had to stop the fight. Compared to that, a win on points was not something fans could call "convincing," and boxing fans like matters settled cleanly and decisively. Then comes the fight against George Foreman in Kinshasa, Zaire (because of the lower income tax there; and, of course, Ali was able to use that fact to win a brilliant ideological argument, for, after all, Foreman, in "reply" to two black athletes who had given the Black Power salute at their medal ceremony in the Olympics, had patriotically swung Old Glory). Foreman is the favorite. People are cautious, but it does seem out of the question that Ali can find his way back to his top form, and particularly against George Foreman, who seems to have everything that Sonny Liston had only promised. Muhammad Ali's victory is another new sensation, all the more so since it was not accomplished by a resurrected "young Clay." On the contrary. For long stretches of the fight, Ali had leaned seemingly passively on the ropes and let Foreman punch away—to the amazement of the American sportswriters, and to the boundless bafflement of the German commentator, and it took Foreman's lying on the mat in the eighth round for the latter to notice that something had been going on here that he hadn't caught on to. The American commentators had realized sometime before that the fight was "turning around."

Now comes a series of inconsequential fights. Against Chuck Wepner (who nevertheless, as we have seen, inspired Sylvester Stallone to play "Rocky"), Ron Lyle, Joe Bugner a second time—two wins on points, one KO. Then the third fight against Joe Frazier. There is no doubt—whatever one's personal preference for one or the other bout may be—that the first fight against Liston, the one against Foreman, and the bout with Frazier in Manila are Muhammad Ali's "three great fights." The Frazier bout was the last of the three—in a certain sense, the most conventional fight and most definitely the one that most resembles Ali's defeats. Liston–Clay and Foreman–Ali are feats of derring-do, and since we find ourselves on the field of martial arts in any case, one could say they were Ali's Lake Trasimene and Cannae.* Manila, however, can perhaps only be compared with Hannibal's having been victorious at Zama.†

But what does a man do with Zama if he wins and is named Hannibal? "This was the next to dying," Muhammad Ali says, and Frazier remarks from his hospital bed that he had landed punches that would have knocked a building down. "What a great champ he is!" In short: it would have been the time to quit. Let's stay with comparisons. One of the few men who could not quit and was the better for it was Augustus, but it turned out badly for Caesar (but then, when should he have quit?). Sulla‡ and Emperor Diocletian were not happy retirees. And let us not delude ourselves. All these retired boxers, whether like Max Schmeling they successfully invest their money in rabbit farms and as tough old codgers live on what they accomplished in their twenties, whether they are found dead in their apartment like Sonny Liston, whether they shoot their ex-wives through the bathroom door like Gustav Scholz, or whether they run a hot-dog stand in Hamburg— measured against what they were before, they all seem a little odd. But how can they help it? Is it any different for tennis pros? Yes, somehow it is. The gap is not so great. The "measured against" is a little less significant. That former life is not half so fraught with atavism and titles. What golf pro would ever have been able

*The sites of two battles in which Hannibal defeated the Roman army.
†The site at which Hannibal's army was finally defeated.
‡Roman general and dictator (138–78 B.C.).

to become a household name known simply as "The Greatest"?

After Frazier, Ali defeats Jean-Pierre Coopman, Jimmy Young, Richard Dunn, Ken Norton—again, just barely (and I admit to having sat anxiously at ringside in New York, and when it was over could only agree with one of the spectators who said, "It was close. Too close to take the title away from a man")—Alfredo Evangelista, Earnie Shavers—all but two of them won on points. Then Ali meets the young Olympic gold medalist Leon Spinks. In poor condition but hoping to be able to rely on routine to manage a couple of fights yet, Ali loses, loses clearly on points. Six months later there is a rematch, and Ali makes good on his prophecy to break Floyd Patterson's record. He is indeed the first man to win the world championship three times; he defeats Leon Spinks, on points, true, but there can be no question as to who won. He now does what he had announced once before after Manila: he steps down. Ali is thirty-six years old. Only insiders and friends— it's hard to differentiate between them—know that he has serious health problems. The next world champion is his former sparring partner Larry Holmes. Holmes wins eight title bouts, one of them against Ken Norton, before Muhammad Ali challenges him. Ali wants to win the title a fourth time. But it seems somehow absurd. To have won it back once is quite a feat, as is to have won it a third time. But what follows is mere infla- tion, or boredom. Why not five times?

Ali is in fact not physically well enough to take on the fight. But he wants to enter the ring, and his entourage from the Nation of Islam urges him on. Medications that dehydrate the body result in short-term weight loss. Ali looks trim and fit when he steps inside the ropes, but it's already over in the first round. The referee doesn't notice anything is wrong, since Ali manages to carry off a desperate act—a parody of himself. Because several of his later fights contained this element as well, no one notices what is really happening: that man standing there in the ring is incapable of defending himself and pretending to be Muhammad Ali. Only his opponent notices. But he doesn't believe it. At last he, too, realizes that his caution is unjustified, that this is not a Muhammad Ali who, however tired, is always capable of bluffing everybody, his opponent above all. Ali has bluffed with that for the last time. Only with that. Holmes glances across to the referee and begs with his eyes for the fight to be stopped. The ref doesn't buy it. And Holmes's greatness consists in his not letting his superiority, which he now suddenly recognizes, to become too clear, as he easily might have done. The fight slows down, turns grotesque, Holmes punches once, twice, three times, again, again. Doesn't the referee see it? After the tenth round, the people in Muhammad Ali's corner see it. They throw in the towel. It's over. I don't know if anyone has ever given Larry Holmes the thanks he is due, not only for having conducted himself in a sportsmanlike manner but also for the decency with which he treated a myth, whom you don't simply knock senseless to the floor. Let those thanks be given here.

And today? Ali suffers not from Parkinson's disease,

as he explains with a friendly, distracted smile, but from "Parkinson's syndrome." His speech is slurred; his hands tremble; after three marriages he is now cared for by his fourth wife, Lonnie, whom he married in 1986. The money—more than any athlete has ever won—has more or less been spent—on what, no one rightly knows. Now that Ali is gone, boxing is the same as it was before, a boring brawl, with a bit of excitement here and there. But with Ali no longer boxing, the fan, the addict, realizes that for all those years he wasn't watching prizefights, but a unique personality, who, let us say simply for lack of a better expression, used a given genre to make his mark in the world. Another genre could have achieved the same effect, but not for Ali, who here had found his genre, and with it compelled people who had never before had any interest in boxing to pay attention to prizefights.

MANILA, IV–VI

A renewed hail of blows to Frazier's head. But Frazier won't let himself be driven to the ropes. "Slower than a tank, faster than the fastest turtle," as Torres once wrote,[29] he marches forward, driving Ali into the corner, dives under a jab thrown too hesitantly and too slowly, lands a left on Ali's forehead, then takes a left hook. But Ali has nowhere to retreat, and Frazier stands with his head pressed against Ali's chest, battering away at his left side below his cover. Ali crumples forward with pain; Frazier, his head now at the same height as Ali's, draws his fist way back. Another punch, which leaves Ali swaying like a tree under the blows of a lumberjack's heaviest ax. There are calls from Ali's corner: for God's sake, get out of the corner! Another two blows—Ali turns, still so close to Frazier that it looks as if they are embracing, and slowly maneuvers his way out of the corner, so that suddenly Frazier is standing almost exactly where Ali just was. Ali shoves Frazier back with both hands and takes a step back himself. Frazier marches forward, and Ali greets him with a right to the head, a left to the head, another left that Frazier fends off, but not the next right and yet another left. "This is a war!" the TV commentator shouts. Frazier throws a massive hook—misses, and stumbles past Ali—a dangerous situation, and he tries to save himself in a clinch. The referee separates them. Ali pulls back again to the ropes, but the previous scene is not repeated. Is Frazier tired? Both fighters move back to the middle of the ring. A few blows from Ali—he, too, appears to be tired. Then the ropes again. Frazier gets through to Ali's chin with a left hook, which is immediately answered by several punches on his part. Frazier lands more punches. He's getting through more often now; Ali's cover is not what it should be. In the middle of the bell, Ali hits Frazier one more time.

During the break, Ali directs the chorus of his fans: "Ali! Ali!" But the next round will be a bad one for Ali. He can't keep Frazier away from him, lets himself be driven into the corner, and stays there almost the whole round. Worse: he tries to fight his way out several times, and doesn't succeed. Frazier keeps driving him back. And Frazier's punches are noticeably more powerful than Ali's. This round is the first one that clearly goes to Frazier.

There is nothing significant about Frazier's catching up; that was to be anticipated from the middle rounds of the fight. But what is disturbing is that Ali is boxing as if he didn't see it coming. As if he had hoped to avoid this turn of events and is now being forced into a rather helpless defensive posture by Frazier. That Ali waves to Frazier once or twice, challenging him to renew his attack, can deceive no one in the audience, and least of all Joe Frazier. And it can't deceive Ali himself, either. Boxing is primarily a matter of lies, José Torres has written: "A fighter lies a lot." What is a feint other than a lie? But Frazier is a fighter you can't lie to. "He is a special machine, a computerized machine which has been fed only with a truth chart. A machine which will reject lies automatically. You can't lie to this machine. You can't fool it with your feints."[30] And Ali can't lie to himself, either. When a kid yells, "Didn't hurt a bit!" he has to believe it—then he won't cry and it won't have hurt so much. But if he doesn't believe it, he'll already be crying when he yells it, and added to the pain will be the shame of standing there humiliated. Ali's gestures are those of a kid who doesn't believe. They don't lessen the pain, and they make Ali look foolish.

At the start of round six, Frazier hangs a mean left hook on Ali's chin, sending Ali stumbling back into the ropes. For a moment Ali holds on to them, but then he pulls away. He tries to keep Frazier at a distance. Now Frazier lands what is perhaps an even more murderous hook. It was this kind of punch that sent Ali to the canvas in the Cooper fight and in the first bout with Frazier. Today it looks as if he saw both Frazier's hooks coming and was able to prepare himself mentally for them. (A knockout never results from just the power of the blow; it also stems from the situation in which a man is hit—from surprise, from a punch that comes "out of the blue.") But if Ali saw these lethal jolts coming, why couldn't he dodge them? The reason can only be that he was no longer physically able to react quickly enough. He can prepare himself mentally for the blow, he will stay on his feet, but he will have to take it, and nothing is going to lessen its power. This means that Ali will take a dreadful beating in this fight, and the question of whether it will end prematurely depends solely on whether Frazier can succeed in so befuddling Ali's senses with his blows that he can either surprise him with one of them or wear down his will until at some point he is no longer capable of staying on his feet when the blow that he sees coming, but cannot parry, is landed.

As before—with the possible exception of round four—Frazier still looks eager to fight. He seems to know that he is engaged in heavy, and ever heavier, work that is painful for him, too, but that will be successful. This is what makes him different from Muhammad Ali, who is presumably grappling with self-doubt during this round, wondering if he will in fact be able to go the distance. Frazier lands several more hard punches in the round—one of them causing Ali to lose his mouthpiece. A minute before it ends, Ali does a couple of what look like light-footed moves, and the commentator notes: "Ali's dancing for the first time!" But Frazier is immediately on the mark with a powerful hook. The end of the round sees a Muhammad Ali who cannot hold Joe Frazier off, and a Joe Frazier who, as Ferdie Pacheco said, looking back on the fight, "was not only fighting with strength, he was fighting with joy."

DEFEATS

W e do not grow from defeat. We are destroyed by defeat, and if not destroyed, then deformed; or we "change"—it is not easy, and perhaps it is not necessary, to differentiate all this very precisely. Defeat does not make us stronger, either. Weakness (whatever its basis) is the cause and effect of defeat. A person can nonetheless be stronger after a defeat than before. But he is stronger in another way than he was at that time and place when he proved too weak. Victories reveal continuity in a personality; defeats necessitate discontinuity. Not because there is something to be learned from defeat. That is not the case. Defeat changes things far too much for us to maintain the fiction of continuity implied by "learning."

Equally foolish are those who "know how to bear defeat." Defeat is unbearable. Only Ajax behaves appropriately: when the weapons of Achilles are awarded to his rival Odysseus before the assembled army, he goes mad and slays a herd of sheep, believing them to be Greeks, and flogs a ram to death, believing it to be Odysseus. He then comes to his senses again, recognizes his disgrace, and kills himself. *He* understood how to deal with defeat, or, if you like, to "bear" it.

Anything but to "survive" it. Whoever has gone bankrupt, got his foot wedged in the ladder, been booed off the stage, been thrashed within an inch of his life in the ring, had his wife stolen from him—they all would like to roar with pain. They cannot endure it. "Endurance" is anesthesia and stupefaction. For the pain comes from damage that can be charged only in part to others—the other part is the uncertainty as to whether you are not justly suffering this defeat. To injury is added doubt, which can suddenly no longer be held in check. The way out of defeat is not to accept it and grit your teeth, but to deal with the inevitability of its consequences and to arrange your life in accordance with the psychological shifts that have occurred. "What doesn't kill me hardens me"—that is nonsense, but it is not nonsense to realize that what doesn't kill you can change your life.

After he regained the world championship the third time against Leon Spinks (the same Leon Spinks to whom he had lost only a short time before), Muhammad Ali retired, and that was the best thing he could have done. For two years he did not box, but traveled around the world, meeting politicians and raising money for charitable organizations, until finally President Jimmy Carter gave him the job of winning African countries over to a boycott of the Olympics (because of the Soviet Union's invasion of Afghanistan). The African countries he visited did not hesitate to make it clear that they found Carter's idea of sending a black athlete to them on a diplomatic mission rather insulting. *Time* called the trip by a political novice like Muhammad Ali "the most bizarre diplomatic mission in recent U.S. history."[31]

In the meantime, Ali's former sparring partner Larry Holmes had become world champion. It is possible that this may have supplied an additional motive for Ali—along with money, publicity, and simply the wish to climb into the ring again. Holmes knew Ali, respected him—and said that in his opinion Ali should not box anymore. That opinion was shared by Ferdie Pacheco, Ali's ringside physician of many years. Ali's health was a matter of public debate, people compared television appearances and interviews, and it was undeniable that Ali's speech was slower and more slurred than only a few years before. His reflexes had got worse as well. The state of Nevada, which licensed the Holmes–Ali fight, demanded a medical examination, and Ali checked into the Mayo Clinic for two days. Ali underwent an exam that found nothing out of the ordinary. Except for the following symptoms: slurred speech, occasional tingling of the hands, trouble touching the nose with the eyes closed, some clumsiness when hopping. But all of it to a very slight degree, sometimes first noticeable or worsening somewhat only with fatigue. Based on that and a small "cavum septum pellucidium" (a hole in the membrane separating the ventricles in the brain), the doctors did not conclude that Ali should not fight under any circumstances, but instead stated "no specific finding that would prohibit him from engaging in further prize fights."[32] The fight could be held.

Ali appeared to be in amazingly good shape. He was as trim as he had ever been since his fight against George Foreman six years before. That, however, was the result of medications that he had been given and that caused the body to dehydrate. He was subjected in general to bungled medical treatment.[33] Even before the fight, Ali had been "an empty shell," as one observer put it. Already in the first round he was exhausted, his reflexes were sluggish, he couldn't dodge punches and could barely land any himself, and they weren't hard even when he did. The medications had affected his metabolism, as well as caused severe dehydration, so that his body could not produce enough sweat. Ali's body temperature kept climbing throughout the fight. Pacheco, who had left Ali before he even began preparing for the fight, because as a doctor he did not want to be responsible for Ali's health, said laconically about the bout: "Ali is lucky he lived through the Holmes fight." According to Pacheco's analysis, Ali could have fallen over dead at any point in the fight. But he didn't. "After the fight, I went to Ali's room in the hotel and told him, 'You're still the greatest; I love you,'" Larry Holmes reports. "I meant it; and I felt awful. I felt terrible before I went to his room, and when I got there I felt worse. Even though I won, I was down. . . . I want people to know I'm proud I learned my craft from Ali. I'm prouder of sparring with him when he was young than I am of beating him when he was old."[34]

You can blame a lot of people for the fact that this fight was even staged. But whom do you blame for its not being stopped in time? Larry Holmes signaled his own confusion to the referee several times; he also spoke with those in his corner about what he should do, since he didn't want to injure Ali. They suggested cutting the misery short and knocking Ali out. It is to Larry Holmes's credit that he didn't try it. Herbert Muhammad, Ali's Black Muslim manager, just hung his head and prayed (he said afterward that he usually did that). The referee did nothing. Ali's trainer, Angelo Dundee, didn't interfere until after the tenth round: "It's over!" Dundee is perhaps the most experienced trainer in the prizefighting business, and he had been taking care of Ali since before he ever became champ. If anyone (besides Holmes and Ali) had to have noticed something, it was Dundee. So that one can hardly blame the ref for not seeing anything Dundee didn't see. But Dundee was not a man to goad his protégés on—though perhaps he was too permissive when they really seemed to want to go on. No, curiously enough, Muhammad Ali should be blamed for this debacle. He fought ten rounds like a stuffed dummy, but in such a way that even an Angelo Dundee (not to mention the ref and the spectators) might think that just maybe "the old Ali" would reappear in the final rounds. For ten rounds Ali—and after all, over the last few years he had fought a series of poor fights that he had only barely managed to win—lied to everyone except himself and his opponent. One of those lies had made him world champion a third time.

Leon Spinks was a young, inexperienced boxer, who had won an Olympic gold medal, it's true, but had only seven professional bouts behind him. The offer of a fight with Ali came from Spinks's handlers, and Ali declined it at first, because he was afraid he would compromise himself simply by getting into a ring with Spinks. Then he began to be intrigued by a publicity gimmick, one that allowed him to grope, so to speak, toward the idea of "retirement": "I beat Floyd Patterson, who won a gold medal. I beat Joe Frazier, who won a gold medal. I beat George Foreman, who won a gold medal. I'm gonna beat 'em all before I retire, to prove I'm the greatest of all time."[35]

Ali had trained very little for the fight, weighed more than he had for any previous bout, and came up against a boxer who might not have been an important challenger but who was well trained, young, strong, and lacking any respect for Ali and who battered away at Ali from the first to the last round without any sign of tiring. It may have been Ali's strategy to make it through the first half of the fight more or less unscathed, so that, or so he hoped, Leon Spinks would tire out and he could then put his experience to use against him in the late rounds. He did very little in the first rounds, but seemed puzzled that Spinks's punches gave *him* a lot of trouble. Ali gave away round after round, and at some point it must have dawned on him that in the end Spinks would have him right where he had hoped to have Spinks: out of gas in the fifteenth, perhaps, and then floored by a sudden flurry of blows. And even if that didn't happen, Spinks would win on points. And so Ali attempted to even the point score. He reminded himself of what the whole world calls "Ali's style," and "danced" all around Spinks, throwing left jabs. And the commentator immediately and obediently responded: "The old Ali"—he meant the young Ali—"is back!" But Spinks was not impressed, and Ali was forced to realize that he would not have the energy to keep moving like that for another five rounds. Moreover, "dancing around his opponent" had originally not been a goal in itself but only the prelude to an onslaught of blows or the point of departure for a quick counterattack. Ali tried the same thing again in the final rounds, especially in the fourteenth, but it no longer "looked good." An unfazed Spinks just kept going at Ali, driving him to the ropes, and Ali didn't lean back into them, as in earlier fights, but almost stumbled or fell backward into them, while Spinks kept up a hail of blows that proved effective more than once. There was hardly a moment when Ali managed to take charge of the fight, to dominate Spinks, let alone to get him into trouble. "It's absolutely heartbreaking," the commentator said, "to watch this splendid man be humbled like this at the hands of a newcomer."

In round fifteen Ali tries to knock Spinks out. It must have cost him terrible effort, comparable to the effort expended in the last rounds of the fight against Frazier in Manila. He hit Spinks a few times—it's not easy to know how hard. For the first time in the fight, Spinks seemed to be truly impressed, stood against the ropes, in the corner, and took punches over and over. Then he pulled himself together and hit back, landing a punch that almost made Ali's knees buckle. Then Spinks rained blows down on Ali again. Now Ali tried once more to turn things around. It was, there's no denying it, a furious round. There were fractions of seconds when you truly thought it possible that Ali might still end the fight in his favor, and there were moments when you thought it possible that Spinks would knock Ali down. None of which happened, and so Ali did not succeed in making up his deficit in points.

When the scores were read after the final bell and one of the judges scored the bout for Ali by a point, the audience booed. The other two judges scored Spinks higher, and "for the first and only time in his life, Ali had lost his title in the ring. He'd been dethroned and beaten up." After the fight, Ali admitted: "I messed up. I was lousy." But: "I don't want to take anything away from Spinks. He fought a good fight and never quit. He made fools of everybody, even me. We all lose in life. You lose your wife; you lose your mother. We all have losses, and what you have to do is keep living, overcome those losses, and come back. You can't just go and die because you lose."[36]

Ali wanted a rematch.[37] "Leon Spinks borrowed my title; that's all," the former champion told reporters. "This is perfect for me. I've learned you got to lose to be great. Think of what it will mean to be the first man in history to win the heavyweight championship three times. That's something I'll have for the rest of my life. Every morning when I wake up as long as I live, whether the sun is shining or it's raining or snowing, I'll be three-time heavyweight champion of the world. That's worth taking some pain and hurt."[38] Ali trained harder for this rematch than for any other fight of his career; he ran three to five miles every morning before breakfast and fought two hundred rounds with sparring partners. It must have been a kind of masochistic exercise, a punishment for earlier transgressions. "All my life, I knew the day would come when I'd have to kill myself. I always dreaded it, and now it's here. I've never suffered like I'm forcing myself to suffer now. I've worked this hard for fights before, but never for this long. All the time, I'm in pain; I hurt all over. I hate it, but I know this is my last fight, and it's the last time I'll ever have to do it. I don't want to lose and spend the rest of my life looking back and saying, 'Damn, I should have trained harder.'"[39]

And fate was kind to him as well. The young Spinks could not understand why he shouldn't enjoy life as the Champ; he broke out of his training camp and took advantage of the fact that there are a lot of women who think a young, muscular, but otherwise somewhat weird-looking man (Spinks was missing his two upper front teeth, making him look like a vampire) can be incredibly attractive when he can call himself Heavyweight Champion of the World and has money in his pocket; he danced the night away in discos and got caught with cocaine.

Ali was in top form, trim, agile, and Spinks looked unsure of himself, had lost the enthusiasm of the underdog who has nothing to lose and everything to gain. "Against Spinks the second time, my plan was simple. Jab, jab, and throw the right hand. If he got in close, tie him up. No rope-a-dope; fight the whole time in the center of the ring. And throw lots of punches at the end of each round. Closing a round right impresses the judges, and I wanted to give Spinks something to remember between rounds."[40] To follow through on that strategy, Ali only had to be in great condition. To upset it, Spinks needed only to do consistently what he had done in the first fight, to apply the classic countermeasures to such a strategy: move in, cut off the ring, fight in close—without getting blocked by clinches. Spinks didn't even have to be a Frazier for that, he just had to be a little better than he actually was. That he had been better in the first fight was due primarily to the fact that Ali had been much worse, that Ali had not presented him with any sort of tactical, let alone strategic, problems to solve. He had let Spinks do what he wanted, and when it came time for him to force his style on Spinks, Ali had lacked both the strength and conviction to pull it off. Spinks had shown Ali no respect, because Ali had not given him any reason to respect him. Now Spinks was standing across from a man who pretended to be "the old Ali" and about whom the amazed commentator said: "This time he's a serious fighter: no messing around, no rope-a-dope, no smiles, no mouthing-off, he's simply getting the job done"—entirely forgetting, of course, that Ali had won back the title the first time from George Foreman in Kinshasa with his "unserious" rope-a-dope, and that all the rest—the messing around, the smiles, the mouthing-off—had been part of "the old Ali"'s style, and that he had in fact lost the previous fight using it. But Muhammad Ali was playing and working at being "Muhammad Ali" the cliché, but with none of the ornamentation that had always got on TV commentators' and sportswriters' nerves. Spinks was confronted for perhaps the first time in his career with a fight strategy—or perhaps with something that he had to take for one—and did not know what to do. All Ali did was to put his routine into play, and he could keep it up because he was in great shape. "Now he's fighting the real Muhammad Ali!" the commentator says about Spinks, and because Spinks believes it as well, Ali wins the fight. That Ali himself does not believe it gives the fight its special atmosphere, part heroism, part irony. A strange mixture.

The fight is what some people would call "postmodern." A simulation, but an effective one, which then calls into question its characterization as a "simulation." Looking back on the fight somewhat later, Spinks said: "The second time we fought, he wasn't better." Which is true, for example, in terms of Ali's punching power. But then why did Spinks look so much worse? "He just held a lot," Spinks added (but that had been the case in the first fight, too), "and I had a lot of things on my mind."[41] And that was the reason. Ali had only one thing on his mind: to make Spinks look worse than he had the first time. Then everyone would think he had fought a great fight. And (to return to the issue of simulation) in a certain sense, he did. How do you differentiate between apparent and real superiority? You can't always and often shouldn't. In any case, the question of what is real and "what lies hidden behind it" is not much help in finding out about every piece of the world. No, the reason why the fight against Spinks was a bad one was that Ali parodied himself in order to win it. Now someone might say, what an ingenious idea, defeating your foe with a parody of yourself. But there's something of the carny boxer about it, too. We want to admire the intentionality with which Ali pulled off his self-parody. But not the parody itself. Everyone who has found his or her way to a certain "style" parodies him- or herself from a certain age on. Bloch's *Experimentum Mundi** is—with a small but important exception[42]—only a parody of (which is not a "variation on") his earlier work. That applies in fact to many other "works of old age." And when that is so, then they simply are not very good, even if they can still impress newcomers. That commentator saw the young Cassius Clay being resurrected in the fight against Spinks. The fans went into a frenzy during the last two rounds, especially at the

*Late work of the German Marxist philosopher Ernst Bloch (1885–1977).

end, when "by unanimous decision" Muhammad Ali became world champ for the third time. While the judge's decision was being read, Ali sat on the stool in his corner—he hadn't sat down during a single break between rounds the whole fight—his face lowered as if somehow in sorrow. The decision is read, somebody grabs his arm and raises it, he is yanked up from his stool, it seems he's being more held up than he's standing, then he pulls his right arm free, looks quickly around to where the camera is running, gazes directly into the eye of everyone watching, and greets his fans by blowing a long kiss. After the fight, Ali retired.

What had worked here, in 1978, and what no longer worked in the case of Holmes–Ali two years later, had almost not worked once before, in 1976. That was in New York, where the third Muhammad Ali vs. Ken Norton fight was held. The first fight against Norton, in March 1973, had been a preparation bout for his second challenge of Joe Frazier, to whom Ali had lost in 1971. Norton was a relatively unknown boxer, and as in the case of Leon Spinks, he was a surprise. Ali lost the fight on points, lost decisively, which was also the opinion of the crowd, who, as they were later to do at the first Spinks fight, booed the judge who gave Ali the win on points. The first fight against Norton was similar to the second against Spinks—here, too, we find a "classic" Muhammad Ali, light on his feet, nimble, firing jabs at his opponent while on the move. The first two rounds had seen one hard exchange of punches; in the third round the commentator says that we are finally seeing the Muhammad Ali who's been missing in the first two rounds: "This is the great fighter, who can neutralize the power of another man's punches with his agility." In fact, Ken Norton had broken Ali's jaw in round two. Pacheco recalls: "The jaw was broken in the second round. . . . He could move the bone with his tongue and I felt the separation with my fingertips at the end of the second round. That's when winning took priority over proper medical care. It's sick. All of us— and I have to include myself in this—were consumed by the idea of winning that fight. . . . But Norton was a guy Ali was supposed to beat hands down, and at that point in Ali's career he couldn't afford a loss. . . . And when we told Ali his jaw was probably broken, he said, 'I don't want it stopped.' He's an incredibly gritty son-of-a-bitch. The pain must have been awful. . . . God Almighty, was that guy tough. Sometimes people didn't realize it because of his soft, generous ways; but underneath all that beauty, there was an ugly Teamsters Union trucker at work."[43]

The fact was that Ali was using this style of fighting in an attempt to stay out of the way of Norton's punches. Now, it takes agility to fight like that, but not just agility. "Float like a butterfly" is nothing without "sting like a bee," and even that is nothing unless the sting is followed by a hard combination. Ali defended himself for twelve long rounds, and hardly ever succeeded in putting together a good attack out of his defensive position. He was protecting his broken jaw. Ali did not look bad, but over the course of rounds Norton's attacks gave him a lead in points scored that Ali could not catch up with. In the break before the twelfth and final round, Ali looked as if he might faint. His seconds massaged his legs and arms, he couldn't move his jaw at all, and it was only with great difficulty that they could reinsert his mouthpiece. He barely made it through the last round, although at its start he went for the impossible and tried to turn the fight to his advantage in the final minutes.

Not six months later, Ali and Norton were in the ring again. Ali wanted to even the score before taking on any other fighters. And in fact—as we learned from the opening of Ali's autobiography—the loss to Norton was the low point of his career. In his loss to Frazier two years before, he had been defeated in a world championship fight, in a fight that had been promoted as "the Battle of the Century," and to lose a fight like that may be painful, but it's still something you can show the world. But who was Norton? It simply should not have been any trouble *at all* to defeat him convincingly. Because he had lost—particularly when you add the bad luck of having had his jaw broken—it should not have been any trouble for him to beat Norton in the rematch. He beat Norton, but he *did* have trouble. Although at first it doesn't look that way. Ali fights to the total satisfaction of most of those who are watching the bout: "He's teaching Norton a boxing-lesson! He outjabs Norton!" and: "What a difference five and a half months make!" Ali provides an almost perfect demonstration for all those who wanted to see a "real Muhammad Ali fight"—on his toes, moving clockwise around his opponent, throwing left jabs, adding his right now and then. For five rounds Norton looks like a tyro. In the sixth, Norton begins to come back, Ali slows down. In the seventh, Norton lets loose a furious offensive that drives Ali from one corner to another. There are moments when Ali looks helpless. Round eight is like round seven. Then Ali moves in for an exchange of blows with Norton. He stands flat-footed in the center of the ring and answers punch for punch. Norton grows more cautious. There's a hint here of what will typify the fight against Frazier in Manila. Ali begins round eleven with a combination to Norton's head, but Norton strikes back, Ali withdraws to the ropes, to the corner, and Norton fires away untiringly. And yet he looks tired. Certain aspects of the fight against Foreman in Kinshasa are evident here. The last round is a fairly wild brawl. The judges score it 2 to 1 for Ali.

Four months later, in January 1974, Ali defeats Frazier on points; in October 1974 he knocks out George Foreman. Eleven months later there is the third Ali–Frazier bout in Manila. One year later Ali is standing in the ring with Ken Norton for a third time. The fight was basically a boring one, without any real high points. Neither Ali nor Norton managed to dominate. Norton punched harder, and it made him angry that it did him no good. In the last round Ali was back on his toes, dancing around Norton, throwing jabs. Twice, but only for a few seconds, Norton was able to mount an offensive. To those watching, this last round seemed almost hackneyed. It was only a show intended to offer the crowd and the judges what they had missed all evening (with the small exception of round nine): "the old Ali." But it's obvious to anybody that whoever has to try to show what he once was is no longer that. It made people uneasy. All the same, Ali won the fight on the basis of the last round, and Norton broke into tears. "The judges always like dancing," was Ali's commentary on the fight.

Let us look at the problem of simulation from the other side. Let us not say that Ali lost or won because or although he pretended to demonstrate what was not (or not any longer) present, but rather let us test the notion that in the cases of Norton, Spinks, and Holmes, Ali knew no other way out than to present an image of himself that they (and all those watching) wanted, detested, feared, and simply expected. And with that we are close to touching the center of psychological heroism—and its intentional use as irony in the second fight against Leon Spinks. The hero remains himself even in the worst storm; the ironist does not recognize himself. In the Norton fights—unconsciously in the first, consciously in the final round of the second—and for the entire second bout against Spinks, we experience moments of the greatest self-alienation, or, if you like, self-discovery. The real *problem* in these fights was that Ali felt duty-bound to his own personality, i.e., to his image in the eyes of others. The hero can take refuge in no one but himself, and if he finds too little or nothing at all there, if "there isn't enough left," he is compromised. The sportswriters emphasized that Muhammad Ali had remained true to himself. What made Muhammad Ali's style exceptional, however, was that it consisted of three very different styles, among which you could not discern any continuities in the sense of a classical "development" of personality. The fight against Liston, which provided the image of "the classic Ali" was style one; the fight against Foreman, style two; the bout with Frazier in Manila, style three. The defeat against Joe Frazier in their first battle in 1971 and the win on points in 1974 were responsible for the switch from style one to style two.

We do not learn anything from victories, but there are, as noted, occasional psychological shifts. Both fights against Frazier are good, indeed first-class, boxing matches, but they are—measured against other Ali fights—conventional. And they follow the same format. Ali attacks Frazier's head, Frazier battles his way through the punches and lands blows to Ali's body, sometimes he gets through up top as well, with a left or right hook. The fight is fast, and slows down toward the end (which is hardly surprising). In both fights there are sequences in which Ali is fleet-footed and rains jabs on his opponent without the latter being able to do much about it, and sequences in which Ali leans on the ropes and gets thrashed by Frazier without being able to do much about it. At the end of the bout, Frazier is the clearly superior fighter, which becomes obvious with the left hook that flattens Ali in the fifteenth round. That was most definitely not the first blow that would have knocked out some other man, a blow that once more proved that Ali—to the detriment of his health—could take more than most men. In his second fight with Frazier, Ali husbanded his energies better and at the end of twelve rounds is the man with more points on his scorecard. But otherwise, the two fights are similar. They are similar above all in the fact that in both fights Frazier is the dominating fighter toward the end, even if he does lose the second. The rhythm of the match is set by Frazier's steady, undaunted march forward and by Ali's sometimes successful, sometimes futile attempts to hold him off. In the second fight Ali managed to land so many punches that he could win. In both fights, however, Ali was not able to turn the fight into *his* fight. There was no escape into self-parody, either, because Ali stopped it himself each time after a few seconds—it was too dangerous.

And so in Manila, Muhammad Ali needed to come up with something else if he wanted to avoid yet another repeat—which would have fallen flat, even in the case of a victory. By the end of the sixth round, he had not come up with anything.

MANILA, VII–IX

In the seventh round we see an Ali who briefly tries to be "his old self." He stands on tiptoe, dances to one side, throws two left jabs and a right, and then Frazier has him on the ropes. Ali moves aside, throws another punch, and Frazier lands a right hook to the head. Ali tries this a few more times, but it doesn't bother Frazier if he has to "chase" Ali, since the chase always ends successfully on the ropes or in the corner, and Frazier can continue with his real work, banging away at Ali's arms, just as his trainer has coached him, getting past the arms to the kidneys on both the right and the left, and attempting at times to get through Ali's defense to the stomach, the head. The commentator, however, is not impressed. "Ali is having a good round." Because what Ali is doing is Ali's style, the commentator sees it as what defines the fight. When in fact Ali is trying to keep away from Frazier. The fight is almost half over.

Round eight. Frazier looks somewhat clumsier, less eager to fight, than in the last two rounds. Something is really bothering him—the tempo of the last few rounds, the punches—or is he, too, starting to notice the climate in Manila—the heat, the almost 100 percent humidity? Frazier throws two hooks, then goes into a clinch that looks as if he were greeting Ali after a long separation. Ali shoves him away but doesn't make use of Frazier's weakness, and instead pulls back almost to the ropes. Then he begins to punch, hard and accurately. The blows hit their target. Frazier backs off. Ali moves a few steps forward. Lands his jabs, again and again. Frazier's face shows not only clear traces of punches landed in rounds past but also a sudden uncertainty. He thought he had the fight in his pocket, and the last few seconds have shown him that's not the case at all. Frazier flails the air with a long left hook, and is hit again. Both boxers are standing in the middle of the ring now; Ali punches and scores.

Suddenly, however, he backs off to the ropes, defenses down. Frazier follows him and goes to work again. A right hook finds its mark. Ali is leaning with one arm on the ropes, as if trying to brace himself, but now he's standing at an angle to Frazier, his cover open. Frazier punches, and does damage. To the chest, the belly, the chin. Ali backs into the corner. Frazier appears to have recovered. His punches are slow and powerful. Ali returns hardly a one. Suddenly they both throw blows at the same time, Frazier a left hook, Ali a right. Frazier lands his, Ali's is deflected by Frazier's arm. Ali is barely defending himself, his cover has dangerous holes. It's the way a man fights when he's taking a beating, or when his thoughts are elsewhere, maybe playing with the notion of how it would be to simply give up and not have another seven rounds of heat and pain ahead of him. Frazier, at any rate, has evened the score on rounds.

Round nine. Ali is barely making any serious attempt to keep Frazier away. A few jabs, pro forma, so to speak. Then the classic image of this fight, an image that we recognize from all the Ali–Frazier fights, but that dominates the last rounds of this fight more than it did any of the others—Ali lets Frazier take over the fight. Now and then a bit of fancy footwork, only to let himself be maneuvered to the opposite corner of the ring again. Despite it all, Muhammad Ali seems remarkably relaxed, which was not the case in the previous round. The imitations of "the old Ali," those few quick steps with jabs at Frazier's head (or in the vicinity), no longer seem helpless, but more like a respite from the pain of Frazier's punches, and the point of each stopover at the ropes seems to be to give his legs a rest. The effect, of course, is like the ultimately pointless attempt of a thirsty man to produce saliva by taking alternate bites of a pretzel and chocolate—but it does seem to work for a little while. The bell.

In the second half of round eight it had become clear to Ali that the moment for turning the fight around had not yet arrived, and his own doubt as to whether he would be in a position to do so if it ever should arrive had almost taken the fight out of him. In the break between rounds, or perhaps in the early seconds of the ninth round, he came to a decision to see this thing through. Ali now fights absentmindedly, and at the same time with concentration. He makes use of his body as if it were a machine that has to hold up under great stress but dares not break down. Maybe this approach also holds at bay the increasing pain in his arms and legs, in his kidneys, his gut, his head.

ROCKY

L et us not speak of "trauma." And yet we are talking about something more than mere annoyance.
Maybe "shock" is the right word? The figure of "Muhammad Ali" was a collective experience that presented the United States with, to put it very neutrally,
problems with which the country had to cope (all this,
of course, in connection with the Vietnam War, in
which Ali refused to serve, and which has openly been
called a "national trauma"). It took five movies, all five
of them huge box-office successes, the first a winner of
three Oscars (and nominated for six more), to cope

with "the image of Muhammad Ali." Sylvester Stallone, the man to whom that task fell (that is, the man who took it on), was, interestingly enough, the same man who had dealt with the "trauma" of Vietnam in his films *First Blood* and *Rambo: First Blood Part II*.

After his fight with George Foreman in Kinshasa, Muhammad Ali had sought and found an easy opponent in Chuck Wepner, a liquor salesman from Bayonne, New Jersey, who was known as "the Bayonne Bleeder" because of his tendency to open cuts when hit. Wepner was the nobody who gets his chance, if only just once. He used it, staying on his feet until the fifteenth round, when the fight was stopped because of Wepner's injuries. But first—and that was the real sensation—Wepner sent Ali to the canvas. Tapes of the fight show that Wepner stepped on Ali's foot just as he attempted to take a step back—but all the same. Wepner later characterized the fight correctly: "I might have been the best heavyweight in New Jersey, but he was the greatest heavyweight of all time."[44] Wepner later landed in prison for possession and sale of cocaine, and it was there that Sylvester Stallone visited him and told him that he was the model for the figure of "Rocky." Stallone wanted to have him play the supporting role of Ching Weber, Rocky's sparring partner in *Rocky II*, but the role was later written out of the film. Looking back: "Fighting Muhammad Ali was the greatest time of my life."[45]

Rocky (speaking for now of just the first film in the series) is the story of a small-time Italian-American boxer named Rocky Balboa, who has never had a big chance, who fights here and there for a few bucks, works as a debt collector for a not-all-that-nasty suburban gangster, and is in love with a shy, nondescript girl who clerks in a little pet store. This small-time boxer is suddenly offered a world championship fight with Apollo Creed, the current black title holder. The reason behind the offer is that Creed's actual opponent has been injured and has had to drop out of a fight that for its hype value has been scheduled for the Bicentennial Fourth of July. All the money invested in PR for the match will be lost if there is no fight. None of the other top ten fighters is available. And then Apollo Creed gets the idea of giving an unknown a chance to fight for the title on America's birthday, for the promise of America is that everyone should have his or her chance. Paging through his lists, Creed comes across Rocky's nickname, "the Italian Stallion"—which doesn't work too well when dubbed into German as *"der italienische Hengst"* and loses any association with the name "Stallone."

Rocky Balboa trains hard for the fight, makes it through fifteen rounds, even knocks the champ down a couple of times in the first round, but in those that follow gets floored more than once himself, only to have his opponent close to blacking out in the last round—when the bell rings, rescuing the champ, who wins on points. The girl from the pet store, who is no longer a shy little wallflower but has blossomed into a beautiful woman through her love for Rocky, even as his own self-confidence has grown, takes him into her arms at the end of the fight, when, exhausted and battered, but happy to have lasted all fifteen rounds against the world heavyweight champ, he says, sinking into said arms: "I love you!"

But let's not deceive ourselves. The film isn't bad. Which is to say: it perfectly meets the requirements of the genre. It does not make the mistake many films do, of cheaply presenting a basically cheap story. The film tells a trivial story with precision, perfection, high production values, and good actors. And here I shall take up cudgels on behalf of Sylvester Stallone as Rocky Balboa: given his blend of naïveté and professionalism, no one could have played *this* role better. The idea and the script are likewise Stallone's. Part of the film's history is that Stallone was still an unknown actor at that point, so that the studio was willing to buy his script but wanted to put a star in the role. The little heroic tale of how, despite all such difficulties, Stallone managed to get his way in the end, etc., is likewise out of place here.

Despite all that and despite the exciting and cleverly filmed fight scenes at the end, the movie would have been just one silly boxing story among many—and presumably would only have confirmed the industry's prejudice that boxing films are "losers"—if Rocky Balboa's opponent, Apollo Creed, had not been all too clearly drawn as the double for Muhammad Ali. The studio is said to have tried to change the script in order not to upset Ali's fans and drive them away from the theaters, but if that's true, Stallone proved to have the better instincts for the film's audience: "Of course Apollo Creed was a thinly disguised impersonation of Ali. If Ali didn't exist, I don't think people would have bought the premise of *Rocky*. But the fact that Ali did exist gave the film validity and pushed it into a believable vehicle for what I wanted to say. And part of what I wanted to say was what Ali represents. I think of him as a manchild, and I meant that in a positive sense. He had a vitality and vigor and drive to topple giants, and that basically is what youth is all about—taking on the icons that have been set before us, toppling old values and trying to replace them with new ones." Stallone emphasizes how much he values Ali, who, after all, proved invaluable to him, and pleads for *Rocky* not to be misunderstood as an anti–Muhammad Ali film: "I was a fan of Ali's. Rambo and some of the other characters I've played are essentially right-wing, but those aren't my beliefs. A lot of people think I'm inseparable from my characters, but that's not true at all. For example, when Ali refused induction, I wasn't as opposed to him as some people assume. I thought Vietnam was an exercise in futility, as most wars are. There were a couple of times I took exception to what Ali said and did. He could be infuriating, but I realized that was part of his psyching. A lot of the time, he was just transferring his own fears onto his opponent. And his fights were a celebration of life."[46] And in one of the early scenes set in a cheap bar, Stallone has his Rocky reply to the bartender, who has slurred Apollo Creed as a "jig clown": "You callin' Apollo Creed a clown? This man is champion of the world. He took his best shot and become champ. What shot did you ever take?"

The figure of Apollo Creed is adorned with Ali attributes, and literally becomes an allegory. Cartoon balloons with original quotes come out of his mouth, and not just talk about "the best" and "the prettiest," about "the Battle of the Century," and so on. At one point Creed quotes almost word for word from a press conference where Ali mocked Joe Frazier for having a son who wanted to become a boxer. My kids, Ali said, are going to go to college and become doctors and lawyers. Creed can be heard to say the same thing in a TV interview. Before the fight, Stallone has the real Joe Frazier climb into the ring and be hailed by the announcer as "Philadelphia's Own Smokin' Joe!" Frazier greets first Rocky, then Creed: "You been dumpin' me a long time." *Rocky* appears in movie theaters less than a year after Manila, but unlike Muhammad Ali's words of praise to the press after the fight in Manila, Apollo Creed calls out: "Joe Frazier! Go home. Don't stay in the arena!" Whereupon Rocky Balboa asks his trainer: "They're friends?"

By way of steering the audience away from falsely concluding that Creed "is" Muhammad Ali, there is the added detail that in his dreary little room Rocky keeps three pets: a goldfish, and two turtles named "Clay" and "Frazier." Adorned with Ali's attributes, Creed is a glorified Ali, an allegory in fact, and the allegorization of a person demands that both he himself and everything for which people believe him to stand assume more or less mythic dimensions. The king or emperor whose robe is painted with goat horns becomes the embodiment of the Devil, if not the Antichrist in person. Creed is the embodiment of some invisible force with definite demonic qualities. Stallone achieves this effect by presenting Creed as "nicer" than Ali himself was. Creed, of course, is not a Black Muslim, he is not even a Black Power man. He is not seriously an ardent patriot, but he uses American symbols (the Bicentennial, the flag) in ways that an erstwhile draft dodger would not.

Indeed, he is notorious for wearing red-white-and-blue shorts in his fights—an interesting detail for helping shape the allegory. The idea originated, in fact, with Wepner, who wanted to add a patriotic note to his fight against Ali. "I'm an ex-Marine, so they played the Marine Hymn as I walked down the aisle to the ring. I was wearing a red, white, and blue robe. It was great." In *Rocky*, however, it is not the title hero but the Ali allegory who wears America's colors and enters the ring costumed as a kind of allegory of the United States—as Uncle Sam, in fact. "I fight for you!" Creed shouts to the fans, an allusion to the "I want you!" of the famous call-to-arms poster with the outstretched forefinger. Creed is therefore an allegory both of Muhammad Ali (who also used to say that he was fighting not for himself but for "America's blacks" or "the ghetto" or "the Muslims of the world") *and* of the United States. For the moviegoer, this is a curious mix, because the man behind the image of Creed had, after all, decided not to fight "for you" in American colors, and even the sentence "I fight for you!" becomes self-contradictory when combined with the gesture of the "I want you!" poster. In short, the allegory is skewed, which is precisely what makes its message unambiguous: this is the false America. The false America is the one in which the image "Muhammad Ali" was/would have been/may yet be the defining image. It is against all this that the film *Rocky* imposes its own images.

But even prior to the images, there is the *name* "Rocky." Recall first that Rocky Balboa, the Italian Stallion, is, like his creator, Sylvester Stallone, an Italian-American. There was a famous Italian-American world heavyweight champion named Marciano; first name, Rocky. Rocky Marciano was champ from 1952 to 1956, when he retired undefeated. After him came Patterson, Liston, Muhammad Ali. Marciano was (with the exception of the interlude of Ingemar Johansson, who was champ for one fight) the last white heavyweight world champion. Here, too, the film is more than clear. Rocky Balboa has a picture of Rocky Marciano in his room, about which his trainer says: "You know you kinda remind me of the Rock? You move like him and you got heart like he did." For a while, in fact, a favorite guessing game among American sportswriters was whether Muhammad Ali could have defeated Rocky Marciano (who was considered the hardest puncher of all time—after, that is, Liston and Foreman had forfeited that title). In fact, they even tried their own kind of "séance." Typical scenes from both Ali's and Marciano's fights were put into a computer, along with everything else that could possibly be programmed into it, and then, since it took time for the computer to come to a conclusion, Marciano and Ali were made to play out scenes for three different endings to the fight. The computer did its calculations and decided in Rocky Marciano's favor. Ali's comment about the result

was to point out where the computer had been built—
Alabama. And now Hollywood had replicated it. Stallone's Rocky symbolized what Floyd Patterson could
not embody: "the white hope" who would bring the
title "back to America."

Above all, to its mythic substratum. Rocky sets the
"false" America to rights again, in that the underdog
becomes "the white hope" and also hands triumphant
black America a moral defeat. Apollo Creed not only
appears, as noted, in the guise of Uncle Sam, but on his
entrance float he also assumes the pose of George
Washington at the legendary crossing of the Delaware.
The announcer calls him the "father of his country,"
and the girls who carry around numbers announcing
the next round after every break are costumed as
Statues of Liberty—and they are all black. Except
that their faces are powdered in silver, so that they
look matte black, like polished metal. A multiplicity
of Miss Liberties, with the number of Apollo Creed's
next round where their torch should be, and the
whole thing staged as the "march of the living dead"
besides. In contrast, white America, the America of
European immigrants—underprivileged, mocked, and
yet proud—rises up, battered and bruised, but indestructible.

Rocky was, as noted, a great success; success breeds
sequels, and so after *Rocky* came *Rocky II–V.* With
Rocky V, then, it's all over—we shall see why. In *Rocky
II,* wonder of wonders, there is a second fight with
Apollo Creed, which Rocky wins this time to become
world champion. In *Rocky III,* coddled and grown soft

with success, Rocky loses his title against an utterly disagreeable black boxer, but then goes on to reclaim it. In *Rocky IV*, he defeats a Russian boxer, who is supposed to show the whole world the superiority of the Soviet system—a film from the Reagan years. In *Rocky V*, Rocky has finally retired and attempts, unsuccessfully, to find an heir to his title. End of series. Each individual film has a clear, almost ritual composition. It begins with the scene of triumph from the previous film, then sets up a new challenge. It is unclear whether Rocky will be able to master it or not, there is a crisis, Rocky overcomes the crisis, and it is always the woman (Talia Shire, who becomes more beautiful with each film) who gives him the final strength he needs. Then, to the accompaniment of pathos-filled music, come scenes of hard training, ending in *I* and *II* in a marathon run up the steps of the Philadelphia Museum of Art, along the beach in California in *III*, and up a Russian mountain in *IV*. Finally there is the big fight, in which victory is in doubt till the very end, and, at last, triumph.

It would not be necessary to discuss the *Rocky* films any further if together they did not have something like a subtext that first becomes clear after you have seen the whole series. It is the transformation of Rocky Balboa into Muhammad Ali. The very image that the first *Rocky* film had "taken the field" to defeat with other images prevails in the end and remains the dominant image. It is not all that easy to figure out just why. But first, the details.

In this regard, *Rocky II* is still restrained. Rocky marries, his wife is expecting a child, the money he earned in the first fight has been quickly spent. Rocky manages just to scrape by in a series of lousy jobs. He wants to box again, because that is the only way he knows how to provide a decent life for his family, but his wife doesn't want him to. Even his trainer argues against it: Rocky is too old already, and besides, one eye has been damaged—"What do you think the champ would do to you? He'd hurt you, permanent!" But Apollo Creed's reputation has been damaged as well; people say he won his last fight only by accident. And so Creed challenges Rocky to a second fight, but so provocatively that even the trainer gets pulled into it: "I think we oughta knock his block off." And Rocky replies: "Absolutely." Rocky's wife: "Rocky." She's wearing a T-shirt that reads BABY. Rocky: "Adrian, I never asked you to stop being a woman, please don't you ask me to stop being a man." That by itself is not convincing, and Rocky trains without any real concentration, is unfocused. Adrian has to be taken to the hospital—a premature delivery. She lies there unconscious for a long time, Rocky watches at her bedside. When she finally comes to, the child—a boy, of course—is laid in her arms, and Rocky says: "Listen, I've been thinking, if you don't want me mixing with Creed no more, we'll make out some other kind of way." Then Adrian says: "There's one thing I want you to do for me: Win!"

And, naturally, things then take their course, especially the training program that Rocky's trainer, Mickey, has come up with. He wants to change Rocky's style completely. Together they watch a tape of his last fight: "See how smooth he moves, how he pumps that jab into your eye. Your style's too easy to figure out. Left-handed fighters, they're the worst. They lead with their faces mostly, trying to throw the big left. Right's no damn good. They oughta outlaw southpaws. To pull this miracle off, you gotta change everything. You gotta learn to be a right-handed fighter. Now this will confuse Apollo and it'll protect that bad eye. But first, we gotta get speed, demon speed, speed's what we need, we need greasy, fast speed!" And so Rocky Balboa remains a man, but is retooled as a machine. Up until the last round, he fights the entire bout leading with his left, and he has become quicker, too, but for the most part he's still the old Rocky. In the last round he's even allowed to be just that, and switches his offensive position. In this fight, which is even more opulently filmed than the first, Apollo Creed is permitted to adopt almost all the poses that we recognize from a wide variety of Muhammad Ali fights. In the last round Rocky knocks Apollo Creed down, but then trips, and both boxers fall to the mat in slow-motion sync, an optical set of twins. Creed cannot get up again; Rocky manages it, in that notorious fraction of a second before the final "Out!" He wins the fight: "Yo, Adrian, I did it!" is the final cry.

Rocky III begins with a reprise of the two boxers falling in sync. Then the story picks right up again where it left off. Rocky, the new world champion, continues to box successfully and on the whole enjoys life, living in a large house with his wife and child, doing commercials for credit cards, appearing on *The Muppet Show,* taking part in a charity match with a wrestler,[47]

unveiling a statue of himself that the city of Philadelphia has erected in his honor. But the audience soon
grows uneasy, for during all of Rocky's bouts, of which
only the last victorious moments are shown, we are
aware of a malevolent black man at ringside who sports
feathered earrings, a Mohawk haircut, and the name
Clubber Lang. In a particularly ugly and offensive
manner, this Clubber Lang challenges Rocky to fight,
and Rocky is ready to take him on, but his trainer
practically forbids him. Since his fight with Creed, he
has fought only carefully selected fighters who posed
no risk, but this man is young and hungry and unpredictable. Rocky insists on fighting, but trains sloppily
and is handed an awful drubbing by Clubber Lang.
During the bout, Rocky's trainer has a heart attack
and dies.

The commentators for the fight, the same pair as in
all the *Rocky* films, are joined this time by Apollo
Creed, who finds some kind words for his former opponent. Then, like the real Joe Frazier in *Rocky I*, Apollo
Creed is greeted in the ring as a celebrity prizefighter.
But Clubber Lang behaves badly even to him: "Get
outa my face. Scram, beat it, I don't need what you got
no more, I don't need no has-beens messin' in my corner, and you better get that bad look off your face
before I knock it off. Come on, come on, you wanna
jump, jump. Come on, Creed!" Creed looks at him for
a long while, then, turning to Rocky, he says: "Give
everybody a present and drop this chump, all right?"
But Rocky loses the fight, and when Clubber Lang is
carried out of the ring in triumph at the end of the

match, the camera pans to Apollo Creed, just as it did to Clubber Lang in Rocky's previous fights.

Mickey the trainer is buried. Night. Rocky, alone and distraught in his training gym. Out of the dark emerges Apollo Creed. "What you doin' here?" "Because I'm the best, and you need somebody to teach you different. To be honest with you, I don't think you can pull it off without me." And then Apollo Creed becomes Rocky Balboa's trainer and teaches him everything he knows. It is the second remake of Rocky the man. If the first Rocky had only one opponent who was his equal, resulting in a kind of parallel identity (cf. the joint fall in sync), Rocky will now become like Apollo Creed. Which is to say: from now on, Rocky will box like Muhammad Ali.

This remake is overlaid with a restatement of "Rocky-should/must-be/become-a-man-again." The training is purposely removed far from all luxury to a squalid neighborhood full of street people and dropouts and the kind of folks who still have a "hungry look" and want to "move up." And so the basic theme of *Rocky I* is reprised. And yet Rocky is once again not quite up to it. The reason: he's afraid of Clubber Lang, he doesn't want to risk everything he's achieved so far, he's afraid that he'll be hurt, if not killed, in the next fight. The shabby world of poverty that Creed has prescribed is not by itself enough. Once again, it is his wife, Adrian, who speaks the word that generates the necessary virility: "If it's over because you want it to be over, I'm glad. It's just you never quit anything since I've known you." "I'm afraid." "I'm afraid, too, there's nothing wrong with being afraid. But it doesn't matter if I tell you, because you're the one who's gotta settle it. Apollo thinks you can do it, so do I. But you gotta want to do it for the right reasons. Not for the people, not for the title, not for money or me, but just you. Just you, just you alone." "And if I lose?" "Then you lose. But at least you lose with no excuses. No fear. And I know you can live with that." "How'd you get so tough?" "I live with a fighter." "I love you."

The fight that then takes place is, in contrast to the fights in *Rocky I* and *II*, which tried to retain some sense of reality, a singular grotesquerie. Not even a caricature of a boxing match can look like this. At first—ringside commentary: "Oh, this is not the Rocky we expected, he's now boxing like Apollo Creed!"— Rocky throws crashing left and right jabs, which connect, and Clubber Lang throws left hooks, haymakers that sound strangely loud as they pass through empty air—"It's absolutely unbelievable, he can't corner the fleet-footed challenger!" Meantime the bad guy, in order to prove how helpless he is, just stands there while the good guy hits him. Thuds and whizzes— "This is Balboa's night!" In the second round Rocky gets beat up a little, even knocked down once, after Clubber flings Rocky into the corner, which looks odd, not like a boxing match at all—"Get out of the corner!" Apollo Creed shouts across to Rocky, just as perhaps Angelo Dundee once did to Muhammad Ali. After being knocked down three times, Rocky staggers about horribly, but then puts both hands to his head and for a moment looks like Muhammad Ali doing his rope-a-dope routine. "Come on, hit me," Rocky says—just like Ali in Kinshasa. In the pause before the third round, Creed asks in shock: "What the hell are you doing?" And Rocky replies: "It's strategy, that's all. I know what I'm doing." In the other corner, while Clubber gasps and pants, his second says: "Listen up, don't go wastin' your punches!" Rocky in his corner: "He's gettin' tired, he's gettin' tired! I swear, I know what I'm doing." Did Ali once say the same thing to Angelo Dundee? And in fact what follows is a fast-forward parody of several scenes from the fight with George Foreman in Kinshasa. Then suddenly comes the same strange gesture Ali made in several fights (especially in the fifth round against Sonny Liston): the left arm stretched out, holding his opponent's head at arm's length. In the real fights, there had always been some point or other to it; here the move looks as if it has been grafted onto the rest of the action merely so that it, too, can be included. Then Rocky challenges Clubber: "Harder, harder, come on, harder!" What follows looks truly awful and is filmed in slow motion, and Adrian lets out a desperate scream: "Rocky!" But then Rocky is suddenly using the Kinshasa double cover and dodging every blow, twice as fast as any boxer possibly could, with Clubber again flailing horribly away at empty air (you can hear the whizzes) and Rocky landing impossibly hard blows (you can hear the thuds). Then there's something like a slapping duel, Clubber takes refuge behind his own double cover, but Rocky, of course, can get through it. Now Rocky follows with an incredibly powerful body blow, for which he holds on to Clubber as if trying to hoist him up a little step-ladder with his fist, and then he knocks Clubber out cold, but goes down with him, in a double fall similar to the one with Apollo Creed at the end of *Rocky II*—but not quite, because Rocky is able to catch himself, lunges past the other man, and exults while Lang is counted out—"What a comeback by Balboa! Rocky is beside himself!" At the end of the film, Creed offers to go a private round with Rocky in the gym, Creed strikes an imaginary bell, and they both punch at the same time, Creed a right jab, Rocky a left cross, and both connect. End of film. Credits.

That final shot shows Creed the equal now of Rocky Balboa, but the succession of images preceding it suggests something quite different. Anyone watching the filmed fight sees, above all else, a new aesthetic arrangement, witnesses an onstage change of scenery. That grotesque fight was something like a re-allegorization of Rocky, already hinted at in *Rocky II* but done in fast motion. Rocky is draped with all the attributes of Muhammad Ali, which had previously belonged to Apollo Creed.

In order to make this re-allegorization complete, Apollo Creed is even made to give Rocky Balboa his trunks. This is—if *Rocky II* is understood as, so to speak, the retarding impulse—the fulfillment of the promise of *Rocky I:* to reconstitute or, if you will, redecorate the falsely constructed, falsely banalized collage of an allegorized America. The curious thing about this image is that aspiring white America chooses the aging boxer, Muhammad Ali, as its father, into whose trunks it now wants to slip. Did Muhammad Ali embody the American dream, as Sylvester Stallone himself formulated it: permanent adolescence, the toppling of one generation by the next? But how can anyone actually do that? Why couldn't the old successful black man simply be toppled by the young successful white man? Why did Ali's image, like some optical illusion, have to be superimposed on that of Rocky, who had served as such a solid counterfigure in the first film?

The image of Muhammad Ali is itself an optical illusion. He was both the bad and the good black man. He appealed to more or less all the ideals the American tradition made available, took advantage of them, and opposed them. He himself was a bundle of all the contradictions that make up his country. His press conferences were pious and blasphemous; he praised America or Africa; he looked forward to going to Zaire and at the same time cracked cannibal jokes; he said the title "Heavyweight Champion of the World" was the most important on earth and publicly advised his children to go to college; he mocked his black opponents, when he wanted to, as submissive "Uncle Toms" or "dumb niggers." During the Olympic Games, George Foreman, gold-medal winner and later heavyweight champ, had waved the American flag. Rocky receives Creed's striped trunks before a fight that contains unmistakable caricatured quotes from Muhammad Ali's bout with George Foreman. And just as it was for Muhammad Ali, this is a comeback fight for Rocky, he regains the title. An allegorical melting pot.

Once Rocky Balboa can do everything Apollo Creed can do, once Rocky and Apollo Creed have become fast friends and Rocky is declared Apollo Creed's legitimate successor by the passing on of the trunks, there is nothing more for Apollo Creed to do in the next sequel. Anyone who knows a little something about dramaturgy would infer the imminent death of the Apollo Creed character, and he would be right. Stallone does away with Creed, but since, unlike in life, one cannot have people leave the stage without some motive, this is managed to considerable effect. In *Rocky IV*, Apollo Creed is killed in the ring. The fatal blow is delivered by a Russian boxer—or better, by a man from the then extant Soviet Union, locked at the time in a cold war with the United States—an invincible fighting machine dispatched to prove to the whole world the superiority of the Soviet (sport) system. The Russian fighter's name was—what? Yes, close guess. His name was: Ivan Drago. Creed wants to show the Russian (and himself, of course) what he still can do, and this time Rocky is standing in his corner. The fight has been declared an exhibition match, and it once again becomes a grand spectacle, even grander than the fight with Rocky. Apollo Creed again appears as an allegory of America, and we have a hunch things will not turn out well. At first the Russian appears to be befuddled by so much Las Vegas glitter—fireworks, go-go girls, and so forth—for although he is a top athlete with a bodybuilder's physique, he spent his childhood (or so we assume) in some lousy village without so much as a fridge or TV. And so in the ring as well, the Russian is not only superior but mean and nasty besides, and in the second round he lands a punch so hard—he knows what he's doing: "If he dies, he dies!"—that it breaks Apollo Creed's neck. After an almost murderous first round, Creed had forbidden Rocky to stop the fight—"No matter what. No matter what!"—and so Rocky waited one moment too long before throwing in the towel.

Apollo Creed is buried; Rocky gives the eulogy and lays his world championship belt on Apollo Creed's casket, then he relinquishes his title and says he will assume it again only after he has beaten the Russian. Rocky's wife, Adrian, is—? Correct: against the fight. And then Rocky says—? Almost correct. He says: "I gotta do what I gotta do." "You don't have to do anything." "I gotta do it." "Before, there were reasons to fight I could understand, but I don't understand this. Even if you win, what have you won, Apollo's still gone. Why can't you change your thinking? Everybody else has to." "Because I'm a fighter. That's the way I'm made, Adrian. That's what you married. We can't change what we are." Then: "You've seen him, you know how strong he is. You can't win." "Ah, Adrian. Adrian always tells the truth. Maybe I can't win. Maybe the only thing I can do is just take everything he's got. But, baby, he's gonna have to kill me. And to kill me, he's gonna have to have the heart to stand in front of me. And to do that, he's gotta be willing to die himself. And I don't know if he's ready to do that. I don't know." Having said these words, Rocky walks out into the night, and as he drives his car through the same night, his whole life passes before his eyes. And we have understood. But just in case we haven't, we are treated several times to the scene where Apollo Creed is knocked to the mat by the Russian, and then suddenly it's Rocky who is standing in his place.

And so Rocky gets down to the hard work of his own resurrection, which, as we all know, first requires a descent into hell. But hell is close at hand: Russia. There, the Russians have determined, is where the fight is to take place, and on Christmas Day, no less. Well, we're not that far along just yet. Rocky takes his farewell from his son: "Remember, Daddy loves you. No matter what," and from his wife—a long look back to the window where she is standing. Cut to: Russia, or, more precisely, the Soviet Union, but since at that time the difference did not yet apply, this is the real Russia. The lousy Aeroflot propeller job lands at a crummy little airport. A polished Mercedes limo brings Rocky and his trainer,[48] Apollo Creed's ex-trainer, to the training camp. And that—"Yonder, they were of course qwarturd in a most wooden hotel"[49]—is a log house in deepest Siberia, buried under snow, without running water or heat. The pump in the courtyard has to be thawed out, Rocky has to chop wood.

In contrast, the Russian's training center: a hi-tech subterranean bunker. Digital displays of something or other, tiny lights, glittering chrome, green video screens with curvy lines, columns of numbers. Ivan Drago trains on ingenious machines that exercise specific muscle groups. And now and then an injection.

Rocky IV is the final and conclusive documentation of the Russia/USSR image with which my generation grew up in the fifties. First, the Russians are cunning. Second, they are hopelessly backward. But third, their technology is superior: T-24, sputnik, SS-20. And in fact: the first man in space was named Gagarin. But what did he look like? Like a World War II pilot. Whereas the American astronauts were always in living color and silvery, the cosmonauts were always in black and white. The masses haven't a crumb to eat, the comfort and service on Soviet airplanes are beneath contempt—but underground, the technology is even more perfect than in the United States.

Of course, we already suspect that in the implied battle of the systems, Rocky's imposed "back to nature" is in fact a "back to the roots"; that he will adopt the American pioneer spirit; and that Ivan Drago, the artificial product of imposed collectivism, will lose. The Russians' trick of banning Rocky to a remote Siberian log cabin will therefore be, as Mao Tse-tung put it, like picking up a rock, only to have it fall on your toes. And that is how Creed's ex-trainer sees it, too, a black man, by the way, for Rocky is meant to represent all of America: "For what you gotta do, it's good. Toughen you up. You're gonna have to go through hell. But in the end I know you'll be the one standing. You know what you gotta do. Do it!" And now the awful training begins, alone in outer Siberia. Cross-country runs through knee-deep snow (and on the road, the KGB limo follows alongside).

The training sequences are edited in crosscut. Rocky saws wood and schlepps boulders, Ivan Drago lifts weights; Ivan Drago climbs a kind of horizontal ladder with movable rungs, Rocky dons a mule harness and pulls a heavily laden sled—etc. Ivan Drago polishes off one sparring partner after the other, Rocky fells trees. All the technological energies of a world power are concentrated on Drago, Rocky helps a Russian peasant pull his horse out of the snow. Finally we see Drago running at full stride around a track covered in some special material, constantly landing blows to a punching bag as he goes. Rocky bears a heavy beam on his shoulders through the snow, his hands wrapped around both ends of the beam, and now his left leg buckles into the snow—but there is no Simon-of-Cyrene-on-the-spot. And back to jogging—Ivan Drago alone on his track, observed by his trainer with a stopwatch; Rocky in the snow, watched by two KGB agents in a black limousine. When he returns home, Adrian is standing at the door of the log cabin: "I couldn't stay away anymore. I missed you." "I missed *you.*" "I'm with you. No matter what." "No matter what?" "No matter what!" Embrace. Then swelling music takes over, and the training goes twice as well and twice as hard. More crosscutting. And we understand yet again: While Ivan Drago drudges away alone in his vast technobunker, Rocky has his loved ones at his side. And his trainer provides the slogan for the fight: "No pain. No pain. No pain." At the end, Drago has to run on a slanted track (in place, no less, and they call that progress!), the angle of which is gradually increased by his trainer (the sadist!). Rocky runs, too. Leaving the black limo behind, he runs up a mountain, while Drago has to run on a track that gets steeper and steeper—then Drago gives up. Rocky is at the top and cries out: "Drago!" It's all fabulously well done, and Hollywood is truly one of the U.S.'s best weapons.

Then comes the fight, which takes place in the largest stadium in Moscow, and it is—what else could we expect?—full of Russians. You recognize them at once, and they all scream: "Drago! Drago!"—you have to be prepared, of course, "for mean shabby Slav=trix like that."[50] And up on a special grandstand sits the entire politburo. We can make out the physiognomy of Andrei Gromyko, and then—to great jubilation— Gorbachev, there's no mistaking him, takes the grandstand. The Russians, being the nasty fellows they are, now provide a counterpart to the show in Las Vegas: a huge portrait of Ivan Drago done in socialist realist style, à la the monument in memory of the Great Patriotic War and the nation's finest tractor driver, rises on the back wall of the stadium to the chords of the Soviet national anthem. The audience, in which one can spot the wizened faces of a good many old generals, rises and salutes. But you can tell that the Russians must have put all the technology at their disposal into Drago's training bunker, because the fireworks that illuminate his portrait are more or less homemade, something like great big sparklers. By comparison with the Vegas show, the only word we can possibly come up with is "tacky." Rocky is wearing Apollo Creed's star-spangled-banner trunks, of course. And what sort of trunks does Drago have on? Red. With yellow stripes. And red boxing gloves, too. Rocky is booed, Drago is cheered. And now the fight of the trunks can start. "I must break you!"

Rocky is dreadfully beat up on at first, naturally, and the fight is even more improbable than any filmed thus far. In the break between rounds, Rocky's second says: "No pain!" But of course the worm turns only slowly. And up in the politburo grandstand, a drama is being played out that surely hints at the course of world history. After the first round, Gromyko glances across in triumph to Gorbachev, who nods back to him: Well done! After the sixth round, however, Gorbachev casts a cold glance at Gromyko, and his stare is fixed as only a Russian's can be. Then comes round eleven. The commentator: "A few cheers, the first cheers for Rocky Balboa. Rocky's determination is actually beginning to win over what was once a hostile crowd!" In the pause before the fifteenth round, you can hear the Russian spectators: "Rocky! Rocky!" Gorbachev shoots another glance at Gromyko, who runs over to Drago's corner and chews out the trainer in Russian (with subtitles): "You trained this damn fool! He's a disgrace!" Then he says to Ivan Drago: "Listen to them. Our people cheer for *him!* Idiot! Win!" This makes Ivan look incredibly fierce; he raises a hand together with Gromyko, lets it fall (and we understand), and calls out (in Russian, with subtitles): "I fight to win! For me!" and then once more, with a raised fist: "For me!" The camera pans to Gorbachev. We can date the end of Soviet collectivism from this point. In the last round Rocky is brutally battered again at first, and then Rocky punches back with incredible power—the enthusiastic commentator: "Rocky Balboa is chopping the Russian down!"—then he knocks Ivan Drago out—"Rocky has done the

impossible, and these people love it! It's absolute pan-
demonium!" Rocky, wrapped in the American flag, is
lifted onto shoulders, and Gorbachev stares at Gromyko,
who hardly dares glance back at him. Then Rocky says
the final word into the mike: It is better for two men
to fight than two countries, and people didn't like
him here, and he didn't like them much, either, but
now that's different, because "during the fight, I seen a
lotta changing. The way you felt about me, and the way
I felt about you. If I can change, then you can change.
Everybody can change!" The sentences are translated
into Russian, and the crowd cheers and applauds. Then
Gorbachev stands up and applauds, and everyone else
joins in, except Gromyko. Then—the fight has been
carried worldwide by satellite—Rocky wishes his son
"Merry Christmas! I love you!"

And with that we have *Rocky IV* behind us as well.
In this film the psychological schema of the Rocky pentad becomes visible, and with it the meaning of the
image of Muhammad Ali. The question "How is it possible for a single man to evolve such extraordinary
effectiveness?"[51] can be studied here anew. As for the
film's individual themes: first we have the same manliness issue as in the other Rocky films. There is little to
say here beyond what has already been provided in the
way of plot and quoted dialogue. The second theme is
political. Aside from the marvelous parade of clichés,
the sheer cockiness of their deployment (two men
carry out the battle of two systems), and the docu-
mented megalomania of Sylvester Stallone (it all must
have been great fun), what is worth mentioning above

all is how the politics are tied in with the manliness theme. Take, for example, the Russian boxer—the Soviet system fails in the end because it develops the wrong kind of fighter(s), men who train soullessly and are sent into battle for an abstraction. These fighters are strong, but heartless. In contrast, the American side produces fighters who have heart, who know what they stand for, who have ideals. These ideals, however, are those of individual self-realization—*the* theme of *Rocky I–IV.* The American boxer is better because he fights for a cause that allows him to fight for himself and only for himself. The Russian boxer realizes this just before the last round—"I fight to win! For me!" Because it all fits together so wonderfully, the ultimately fully absurd escalation of the Rocky material to the level of world politics comes across as strangely plausible.

But the Rocky saga was hardly apolitical from the very start. There was the Bicentennial of the founding of the United States, Apollo Creed in the pose of George Washington. Rocky has become an international politician in *Rocky IV,* but he was always a national political figure. In *I* and *II,* he regains the title for the "real" America and fights against the "false" one. And the "real" America was to be discovered again where people know their roots and are not yet sated, where there are people for whom everything is not bluff and show, people who still want something and are prepared to risk their necks for it—people, that is, who are fighters. The "false" America was to be found among hypocritical slickers, where the ur-American offer of giving everyone a chance is only an advertising trick, where the flag has degenerated into a promotional gag. In *III*, Rocky himself fell victim to the false America, to his false self—he first became soft, then fear took over. And he had to become authentic again, return to his origins, so that he could renew the battle with a "false" America. In this case, "false" America was the "bad black America" that Apollo Creed, with several of his Muhammad Ali attributes, had likewise represented in *Rocky I*, but it is now represented by the even darker figure of Clubber Lang. Whereas Rocky is the spokesman of the "good lower class," the goal of which is to move up in society, and which, if it tries hard, does just that (while new lower classes arrive as immigrants, climbing the ladder and repeating the cycle through the centuries), Clubber Lang is the representative of the "bad lower class," which doesn't want to make it to the top, but wants instead to destroy what is above it, simply for the sake of destruction. "This time," he says in a TV interview, "there won't be no quick knockdowns. I'm gonna torture him, I'm gonna crucify him real bad!" (It was said of Ali, and perhaps correctly, that he kept some opponents, those who had insulted him, in the ring and on their feet longer than necessary. Some of these traits have been inserted here.) And Clubber Lang almost succeeds, too, in destroying Rocky's happiness as an upwardly mobile family man. Only when Rocky once again avails himself of the virtues of the "good lower class" does he win, and Clubber Lang vanishes like a wraith. To be sure, Rocky cannot manage it without the help of the "good black man," which Apollo Creed has now unambiguously become, teaching Rocky Balboa everything he knows so that he can defeat the "bad black man."

But the alliance of Creed and Balboa is not only an alliance of the good black America and the good white America against bad black America, but it also occurs on another level. What did Adrian say? "Even if you win, what have you won, Apollo's still gone. Why can't you change your thinking? Everybody else has to." What is the purpose of changed thinking? With whose death must every man reconcile himself? Yes, quite right. And now listen to Rocky as he gives the eulogy for Apollo Creed: "There's a lot I could say about this man. But I don't know if it matters now. I guess what matters is what he stood for. What he lived for. And what he died for. You always did everything the way you wanted it. I didn't understand, but now I understand. I'll never forget you, Apollo." These are things a son might say at the grave of his dead father, that is, if their relationship has not been the best. Love and guilt. And Rocky adds: "You're the best!" Father is the best of all. And the Greatest. Rocky takes off his championship belt and gives it back to Apollo Creed. After all, he had previously beaten the man whom he now adopts as his father, robbing him of throne and title. Rocky not only appears as the avenger but also subjects himself to self-imposed punishment (leitmotif: "No matter what"—and his wife can again take her place at his side, if she accepts this). After punishment and revenge have been carried out, Rocky can again take an idealized stand at Apollo Creed's side—or shall we say, a seat: at his right hand.

And what also now becomes clear are both the motivation for the exaggerated "become-like-Apollo-Creed" in *III* and those grotesque fight scenes in which Rocky is re-allegorized. When Apollo Creed offers to train Rocky, the latter has already undergone punishment and been "almost killed" in the ring. Anyone comparing the scene in which Ivan Drago breaks Apollo Creed's neck with the one in which Clubber Lang knocks Rocky out will find that they are practically identical. In *III*, Rocky suffers punishment for slaying this "father," Apollo Creed. But why should Creed be the man who symbolizes Rocky Balboa's father? For indeed there is no trace of it at all in *I* and *II*. We perceive it only ex post facto, after those strange spectacles of *III* and *IV*. Perhaps one can say that only retroactively does Apollo Creed become a father in the first two films.

As Rocky is standing, punished and beaten, all alone in his training gym—he has just come back from the site of his blasphemous self-elevation, the statue erected in his honor, where he muttered silent curses—Apollo Creed steps out of the darkness like a ghost and makes his offer to train him: "I don't think you can pull it off without me!" Indeed, Rocky doesn't even recognize him at first—Hamlet's problem. The way out, the path of mortification and punishment which the ghost offers him, is the classic "Become like me!" We, along with Freud, don't want that to sound silly: "Even the great Goethe, who in the period of his genius certainly looked down upon his unbending and pedantic father, in his old age developed traits which

had formed a part of his father's character. This outcome can become even more striking when the contrast between the two personalities is sharper. A young
man whose fate it was to grow up beside a worthless
father, began by developing, in defiance of him, into a
capable, trustworthy, and honorable person. In the
prime of his life his character was reversed, and
thenceforward he behaved as though he had taken this
same father as a model."[52]

By identifying with the father, one has the chance to
escape one's sense of guilt and fantasized fear of punishment. When viewed from *III*, then, *I* and *II* are
enactments of patricide, which are "healed," as it were,
in *III*. Rocky now holds the title of world champion,
but something else remains: the title of being "the
best," "the Greatest." Rocky remains the unworthy
pretender to the throne, the usurper. And so in *IV*,
Apollo Creed must die once more—which is very like
an attempt to prove that Rocky could not possibly be
the true murderer. Then Rocky gives the title and its
trophies back to Apollo Creed. He takes the field of
battle as Apollo Creed's representative on earth. In
fact, Rocky is much like the founder of a religion; he
does what Freud describes in *Moses:* he does not set
himself in the place of the father, but rather elevates
the father to a position among the gods and dedicates
himself to his service. And once again, looking back
from *IV*, we see that the identification in *III* was a
renewed transgression.

Before turning at last to the question of what
Muhammad Ali's image has to do with this peculiar
expedition into the realms of mythology, let us cast a

worried glance back to the end of *Rocky IV*, which shows Rocky's absolute triumph, shows him there in the heart of Moscow, wearing his striped trunks, wrapped in the star-spangled banner—and not, for instance, his returning to the grave of Apollo Creed. Psychologist and mythologist would agree that this cannot come to any good, any more than did Moses' hubris in the desert. And it comes to no good, for a fifth *Rocky* arrives in the theaters. It begins, as have all the others, with the final scenes of the preceding film. Now we see Rocky Balboa under the shower in Moscow, then sitting tired, exhausted, and battered on a wooden bench in the locker room. He calls for his wife, who comes; he shows her his hands, they are trembling uncontrollably: "I can't—I can't stop my hands from shaking." Back in the States, Rocky has a checkup, and the results show not only that his hands are trembling—like Muhammad Ali's—but also that he has a hole in the membrane separating the ventricles in the brain—like Muhammad Ali. Perhaps the result of too many too powerful blows to the head, but at any rate reason enough to never box again. A reprise of the theme of punishment and identification. Moreover, Rocky is poor. Corrupt advisors have ruined his fortune while he was in Moscow. Here, too, reminiscences of Muhammad Ali. Rocky must return to where he came from, but in this film, that doesn't mean "back to the roots" for a new climb to the top. It's over. Moses stays behind in the desert.

But a young boxer, Tommy Gunn, who wants to make it to the top, seeks out Rocky's advice and help. The first fight that finds Rocky standing in his corner takes place in the same cellar where we saw Rocky fight for the first time in *Rocky I*. Then Rocky guides him from bout to bout, until he gets a shot at the world championship. And Tommy Gunn boxes just like Rocky, of course. The press refers to him as "Rocky's boy," even as "Rocky's clone." Rocky even lets him wear those striped trunks. But Tommy Gunn is unworthy. He lets himself be bought by an unscrupulous black boxing promoter who, even though he has been informed of the state of Rocky's health, wants nothing more than to lure him back into the ring. The promoter gets Tommy the championship fight. He wins and then is publicly heard to say, as Rocky watches the proceedings on TV: "I want to say thank you, I'd like to thank the man that made all this possible . . ." Cut to: Rocky, smiling a slightly embarrassed smile. Cut to: ". . . the man who made me believe that all this could happen . . ." Cut to: Rocky smiles some more. Cut to: ". . . Mr. George Washington Duke!" He is referring to the unscrupulous prizefighting promoter.

The rest can be told quickly. George Washington Duke tells Tommy Gunn that he will never be accepted as heavyweight champ unless he fights Rocky. Tommy Gunn at once drives to see Rocky, then bad-mouths him, and it ends in an alley brawl among garbage cans, which Rocky wins, of course. And with that he has triumphed over his own clone—or his false self. For not only has he taught Tommy Gunn "everything I know," just as Apollo Creed once taught Rocky Balboa, but he has also identified himself with Tommy Gunn. During the broadcast of the championship bout, Rocky is so "into it" that he punches a sandbag in the same rhythm with which Tommy is working over his opponent, and they both simultaneously fire the decisive knockout punch.

But what happens when Rocky does in his "false self," which is in actuality only his real self, that is, his self before the point when he clones himself as the second Apollo Creed? Rocky vanishes. He will box no more; his identification with Apollo Creed has already vanished, for none of that is part of his training of Tommy Gunn; finally, then, the double of the early Rocky vanishes as well. What remains is the direct identification with Muhammad Ali: trembling hands and brain damage. And something else, too. At the end of the brawl with Tommy Gunn, Rocky knocks down George Washington Duke, who happens to be present. This is not just another "bad black man" (he is that, too), but, above all, a clear embodiment of the most famous black boxing promoter in so-called reality, Don ("Duke") King.

Don King was not merely the promoter for many of Muhammad Ali's bouts, he was also the promoter for the Muhammad Ali–Larry Holmes fight. In Hauser's Ali biography, we find the following quotes:

Mike Katz: "I just know that it was essential to Don King for Ali to go ahead with the fight. This was one of the few times King had his own money on the line, as opposed to someone else's. If Ali–Holmes had fallen through or failed at the gate, King would have been in trouble. And of course, it was clearly in Don's interest to have Holmes win. He was Larry's exclusive promoter."

John Schulian: "I hated Don King for promoting that fight. . . . You didn't have to be a rocket scientist to know at that point that Ali was facing brain damage. He wasn't talking the way he used to. . . . And Don King; that lying thieving motherfucker. That he could stand there and say, 'Oh, Muhammad; I love you, Muhammad. I'm with you, Muhammad; you're the greatest!' And then make a fortune off Ali getting brutalized that way. Well, fuck you, Don King."[53] And the film *Rocky V,* and with it the entire pentad, ends with the same "Fuck you, Don King!" No sequel is possible, the story is over. On the surface of the story, Rocky plunged forward from success to success, until the taking of Moscow—then came the great fall. At the level of images, or let us say, the films' level of implicit mythology, we see something else prevail. At the start, there is the image of Muhammad Ali, which is to be supplanted by that of "Rocky," but in a constant stream of new allegorical thrusts, the image of "Rocky" takes on the contours of Muhammad Ali's image; this allegorical redecoration, however, is then cast aside as blasphemous, Rocky becomes the servant of the image, and when, despite all the excesses of self-punishment, he proves unworthy of it, Rocky obliterates himself. All that is left is the identification in suffering—and the desire to punch Don King in the nose.

Bell—so to speak. All on its own, the last film has brought us back to our topic and to the question posed previously: "How is it possible for a single man"—we are speaking here not about some destroyer of worlds or any other of the classic "great men," but simply about a boxer, who was paid to pummel other human beings—"to evolve such extraordinary effectiveness?" No portion of what makes up the image of Muhammad Ali would be conceivable without his boxing matches. This is not a trivial point, for it means the reverse is also true: Had he been only a boxer (and not a PR genius, not a loudmouth, but also not a Black Muslim, not a conscientious objector, not the author of screwball poetry, not the man in whom Bertrand Russell, Martin Luther King Jr., and Malcolm X were interested), he would have been famous all the same. He would not have been the person the United States destroyed to the extent it did in the sixties, but he would have been a famous boxer nonetheless. What is more: Muhammad Ali's traits as a boxer dominate and imbue all the other parts of his public image. And even if the latter, in and of itself, is nothing more than glistening sparks from some sort of advertising fireworks, behind it there lies—in a bleakly archaic way, to be sure—the battle with fists, the measuring of a man's strength and stamina, and all that modern PR superficiality is stamped with a seal of prehistoric quality. Therefore, once more, whoever wishes to understand the revered, loathed, admired, despised (and the list of adjectives can go on for a long time) image called "Muhammad Ali" has to investigate the style of Muhammad Ali the boxer.

Muhammad Ali was suitable for use as a role model in the *Rocky* films for two reasons. First, because of his *Proteus-like quality.* Anyone who observed him over a longer period of time could find in him something that looked like a piece of the observer. Second, because of his unconditional will for *dominance*. In Muhammad Ali's defeats one can see that both sides *had* to merge if he was to be successful. From his victories one can learn what was so fascinating about him when both sides *did* merge.

MANILA, X–XII

R ound ten. A tired round. Ali punches pro forma.
Frazier just keeps on going, too. With no great
enthusiasm. Ali is exhausted; his timing is off; this
would be the time to land a decisive blow. A round can
hardly be any slower than this. Both boxers lean on
each other, Ali on the ropes, Frazier on Ali. Frazier
pulls himself together to throw a punch that Ali half
blocks. Pause. Then Ali feels it's his duty to try a punch,
and he connects, but so feebly that Frazier quite correctly doesn't even make the effort to parry it. At one
point Frazier raises his cover in the expectation of

a counterattack that never happens. When Frazier punches and hits, he hits far harder than Ali. (The commentator: "That did Ali no good!"). But how is the fight, or simply this round, supposed to go on? Both boxers look as if they've fought themselves out—not just tired but listless. And this can drag on, these two men can drag on like this to round fifteen—but no one wants to see that. Bell. But if you use the slow-motion button on your video remote to watch the round again, you can see the drama, the adventure in the doldrums. You see how the punches that hit home add up, how each man is wearing away at the physical and psychological substance of the other. Not when the fight is all over, but here in the pause between rounds ten and eleven, Ali says to his trainer, Angelo Dundee: "Man, this is the closest I've ever been to dying." He makes the remark, however, not in resignation but as an announcement of a transformation.

In the eleventh round Ali comes out fast, fleet of foot, hard of punch. Frazier has his back to the ropes. Ali connects. Not hard, but something begins to change. Then a hard left-right combination that Frazier absorbs, and yet suddenly he has Ali backed into a corner again. The referee separates them. Ali lets himself be driven to the ropes once more, but only briefly. Then he leaves them—and it is a remarkable gesture. With his left hand on the back of Frazier's neck (one of Muhammad Ali's preferred techniques for blocking an opponent), he pulls away in an old-fashioned spin that looks like some move out of an eighteenth-century dance. Ali jabs, but sparingly. The time has not yet come, whatever the criteria for that may be, but he jabs precisely and no longer pro forma. He gives Frazier the signal for the final portion of the fight. Then he is standing in the corner again, almost immobile, and lets Frazier do his lumberjack work. The end of the round is like the beginning. An announcement that the fight has turned around.

Round twelve. But at first there is no sign of a change in direction. After a flurry of blows, Ali is back on the ropes again, in the corner. But then precise and hard combinations get through to Frazier's face. Frazier punches with everything he has, right into Ali. Ali scarcely defends himself. He pushes Frazier off but makes no attempt to get out of the corner, only seems to be looking for a little air. Now Ali changes corners, spins out of one, and pushes himself along the ropes to the next. Frazier follows and goes to work. Muhammad Ali leaves the corner as if Frazier were a guest to whom he is saying good-bye. There's such friendliness in the way he lets his left hand drop from Frazier's shoulder—Frazier is suddenly standing alone in the corner. The rest of the round is a grappling match with punches, Frazier finds himself on the ropes, then both boxers are in the center of the ring. Bell.

VICTORIES

Victories have something self-evident about them and therefore are often boring. There is nothing duller than a boxing video entitled *Boxing's Greatest Knockouts*. When you write about victories, your writing style takes on a teleological tinge. And even when you want to avoid it, you fall easily into artificial drama. Hopes and fears are silly in retrospect. Far better instead to lean back in your armchair and like some Hegelian historian demonstrate how it all had to happen this way. At least in the case of boxing, you don't have to reach for all too ponderous hypotheses, but can simply talk about the winner's strategy. And that is what we'll do.

Miami Beach, 25 February 1964. "Before the bell for the first round that evening, February 25, during the pre-fight instructions, Liston stood in the center of the ring trying to stare the challenger down. Towels tucked under his robe to give his big frame an even more awesome appearance, Liston attempted to intimidate Clay as he had so many others, but Clay stared right back at him and repeated over and over, 'Now I've got you, Chump.' Then the fight was on. 'He was shuffling that way he does, giving me the evil eye. Man, he meant to kill me, I ain't kidding,' Clay described it to me years later."[54]

Liston believed about himself what the whole world believed about Liston: that he was the most dangerous, most powerful, and perhaps the best boxer of all time, that the young Cassius Clay was nothing more than a loudmouth who was "scared to death." When asked by sportswriters how long he would be able to last against Liston, Clay had replied: "I'm young, I'm pretty, I'm fast on my feet, I look good and I can't be beat." Having been told what Clay had said, Liston merely replied that Clay maybe looked good now, but not for long. Then came the famous weigh-in scene, which seemed to prove to everyone that Clay really was crazed with fear. Liston, however, came away with the unpleasant feeling that he would have to climb into the ring with an unpredictable madman. Granted, that probably only increased his determination to finish the fight as quickly as possible.

Bell for round one. Liston goes for Clay, who dodges. Liston takes two more steps, Clay is already elsewhere. In fact, that image is typical for the whole first round. Liston tries in vain to catch Clay, dancing elegantly on his toes around Liston, who holds his hands almost provocatively low. On second glance, however, the scene looks a bit different. Fairly quickly Liston lands a jab to Clay's body, at about the level of the heart. The heart area is among the classic "KO spots," since a blow there can lead to temporary disruption of the heart's rhythm and a general circulatory collapse. Nor is it true that Clay wants to demonstrate his superior elegance to the crowd—though it may look that way ex post facto. But on closer look, you notice that Clay is being incredibly careful. That first blow showed him that Liston is indeed dangerous. Clay is not full of self-confidence, but rather first has to gain that self-confidence in the ring with Sonny Liston, and to do that he has to make it through a couple of rounds.

Liston misses twice with a wide-arched hook, stumbling in the process, pulled forward by the inertia of his swing. Clay throws two left jabs that connect. Then Liston has Clay on the ropes. Clay bobs down and simply slips right past Liston without his even noticing. It looks funny, and Liston begins to resemble the klutz that Clay's propaganda was intended to make him appear. Clay is obviously pleased as Punch by his trick, he does a little hop and jump—at a safe distance. Liston misses again with two, three hooks, then he tries with jabs. Clay is no longer dancing to the side, but tries something new. He stands still and dodges with just his head, now left, now right. It works. Liston can't hit him even then. Meantime there are two jabs from Clay, then a left-right combination. More long jabs from Liston that connect with nothing but thin air. And suddenly a combination of six blows—you really have to say—explodes at Liston's head, a right jab, a left hook, a right, two lefts, another right hook. Three steps. Another left-right combination. Two steps. Left-right-left. The round ends with long, scorching lefts to Liston's head.

It is a fact that in this first round Liston hit Clay first, not vice versa. It is also a fact, however, that it was the only punch Liston landed. Whereas Clay surely hit Liston more than twenty times. That Clay proved faster and more agile than Liston was no surprise, it was obvious. But it was obvious as well that Clay could make a fool of Liston whenever he liked. Equally obvious was the fact that Liston was boiling over with rage by now. And that a blow like the one at the start of the round could determine the fight.

Looking back at this fight also requires a correction to the legend of Clay's style. Clay did not circle Liston, covering him with left jabs "to wear him out," in order to finish him off with a right when opportunity knocked. Whoever sees Clay's boxing in that fashion is seeing only the cliché that results when Clay's style is adapted to the classic boxing style, in which the right-hander leads with his left, in order then to exploit some awkward defensive move by his opponent and try to knock him out with his (stronger) right. The secret (although it's patently evident) of Clay's (and Muhammad Ali's) style, however, is in the "combinations," i.e., a series of punches. A KO, as I've already noted, seldom occurs because of the sheer power of the blow. It is, as José Torres pointed out, a question of timing. A KO is usually achieved by a punch that the opponent cannot prepare himself for. There are punches that you cannot parry but that you still see coming—and you can prepare yourself for them. But not for a "bolt out of the blue." With his quick combinations, Clay/Ali attempts to *precipitate* a KO situation instead of waiting for it as a gift of chance. In a quick combination of punches, there's always at least one for which the opponent cannot prepare himself. If it is hard enough and connects in the right spot, there is a good chance of a knockout. Whoever can cover his opponent with a *combination* of landed punches has established total dominance for that short period. While other boxers have a favorite punch and are always trying to deliver it at the right moment, Clay's style is directed at achieving such moments of *dominance*. Clay's style is organized around his goal of quick combinations of hits, without favoring any particular punch or favoring one lead hand over the other. This goal also causes him to hold his hands low, which boxing experts have so often found fault with. This is not done to provoke the opponent—that would be childish. Anyone who really observes Clay realizes that he is not simply holding his hands low, but in constant readiness. They are always in motion, not raised in the "normal" way to provide a better defense from behind which punches are then fired. His hands are always ready to make use of the chance for a one-two combination, whether Clay is holding them low or high. Clay's hands are positioned for attack and not for defense. Granted, Clay *very* often does hold his hands low, and for one simple reason. In this way he keeps them out of the field of vision of his opponent, who is, in fact, watching the head and upper chest, because first, that is where he wants to hit, and second, that is where his opponent's fists usually are. Clay, however, keeps his fists out of view, thereby making them less predictable. Although they have a longer path to their goal from below, they are (quite apart from Clay's physical speed) psychologically "faster," so to speak. Of course it's dangerous. But with his quick legwork and his ability to dodge blows with his head, Clay can compensate for the risk that comes with neglecting defense in order to be ready for a surprise attack. For traditionalists, idiosyncrasies. But the peculiarities and, indeed, the mistakes in Clay/Ali's style result from Clay/Ali's always working toward one goal: the sudden combination, the moment of absolute dominance in the ring. For those who understand that, all else follows. Only this one goal is important; everything else is subordinated to it, and is therefore *variable.* In and of itself, it is not important to be "fast on your feet," to "dance." That can be a tactical element in the service of the strategy, but it need not be. That is why it was such nonsense when in the last round of the third Norton fight the commentators saw "the old Ali" resurrected. The "dancing" was there in order to *hide* the fact that Ali no longer saw any chance of using a successful combination against Norton. That is why his "dancing" was not part of the Ali style but rather self-parody and bluff. In the fight with George Foreman (about which we shall have to go into greater detail), there was not a single interpolated dance, yet it does indeed contain a series of impressive combinations. When Ali won big and convincingly, he succeeded in organizing his style around the goal of combinations, and then in varying it—depending on his opponent—indeed, if need be, in apparently revising everything totally. The fight against Liston shows the "agile" Clay/Ali, the fight against Foreman the "immobile" Clay/Ali. And in this union of end and means, *dominance* and *variability,* we again find the boxing style that has made the image of Muhammad Ali so fascinating for so many people, and that caused Sylvester Stallone (and millions of moviegoers) to plug away at it for five long films.

Round two. Clay throws two hesitant lefts, Liston counters with a quick left hook to Clay's head. Clay steps back too late but doesn't show any effects. Clay is not dancing but standing flat-footed. Liston has grown more cautious, he is no longer trying to direct wild swings at a target that is constantly evading him. Except for that one landed punch—and even with it Liston did not succeed in doing any damage. But Clay, too, stays more cautious and calmer throughout the round. For good reason. No one could keep up the tempo of that first round for long.

Round three. Two punches by Liston—too slow. Clay punches back. Then Liston suddenly finds himself in a

veritable thunderstorm of blows. A left, a right, Liston
bends low to get out from under the blows, comes back
up, and is met with a left hook. Clay bounds a good distance away, then comes forward again, a left jab, a right
hook connect with Liston, who has returned to a
crouch, then Clay is above him with two left hooks in
sequence, another, a right hook, another—three, four
more blows connect. Liston reels for a moment, pulls
himself up, lets himself fall back into the ropes, and is
met with a right jab, followed by a left, tries to punch
back now, but Clay is out of reach, a left lands a good
eight inches short, and Clay hurls a taunt of some sort.
Another one of Liston's punches goes wide. Then Clay
is back at his opponent, one-two, one-two-three, one-
two, and one of these punches connects with the hinge
of Liston's jaw. Clay jumps back, and now there follows
a long sequence in which Liston chases after him, trying in vain to hit him. But then, it's not clear just how,
Liston has Clay on the ropes, and Clay can't wriggle
out of it this time. Liston strikes, once, twice, then Clay
checks him by going into a clinch. He holds Liston so
tight that he can't get a punch in. Liston wants out, but
Clay won't let him, using his right arm to wedge Liston's left tight while blocking Liston's other hand, too.
The referee separates them, and Clay moves back. The
round is half over, and the commentator notes that Liston's face is showing traces of battle, a cut under the
left eye. Clay, later: "The blood spurted right out. I saw
his face up close when he wiped his glove at that cut
and saw the blood. At that moment, let me tell you, he
looked like he's going to look twenty years from now."[55]

In the second half Liston manages to hit Clay three times, once with a powerful punch. Clay has to go into a clinch for a moment, then he takes refuge on the ropes, both hands raised to his head—like a prelude to those later fights in which he spent entire rounds in this position, calling it "rope-a-dope." Clay's speed and agility, his ability to dodge Liston's haymakers, make it easy to forget that he did not always succeed. Clay proved early on, though it was hardly noticed, that he had a considerable capacity to "take it." Anyone who observes how he manages to take Liston's few but powerful blows with almost no evidence of impairment will show no less respect but considerably less amazement upon learning that for thirteen rounds against Ken Norton, Muhammad Ali fought with a broken jaw; nor will that observer ever suggest that Ali acquired the ability to "take it" only later on, not when he watches Ali take a blow that literally knocks him off his feet— and would have sent other men into a coma—and be on his feet again before the referee even begins the count. Everything Muhammad Ali showed, had to show, in his later fights was not just already "latent" in the young Clay, but those same abilities were also extant and he knew how to use them. Clay's youth and greater agility did not yet require that they be brought into play as decisive factors in the fight. Whoever watches the Liston fight in slow motion can recognize all the later fights already—but in minimal sequences. The elements of the fights did not change, but their arrangement did. The arrangement, however, determines the physiognomy of each individual fight.

In the fourth round Clay gets hit again, and by the end of the round he is not boxing with the same sovereignty as at the start. He begins to blink nervously. In the pause for round five, there is a sudden crisis in Clay's corner, the cause of which has never been definitely explained—much to the joy of all sports detectives. Angelo Dundee: "Near the end of the fourth round, Cassius started having trouble with his eyes. To this day, nobody knows exactly what the problem was. It might have been liniment from Liston's shoulder. My guess is, it was the coagulant his corner used on cuts. Probably, Cassius got the solution on his gloves, and when he brushed them against his forehead, it left a layer of something that trickled down with the perspiration into his eyes. Whatever it was, he came back to the corner after the fourth round and started shouting, 'I can't see! My eyes!' And something was wrong. His eyes were watery. He was saying, 'Cut the gloves off! We're going home!' And you can imagine what was going through his mind. He was winning the fight, winning easily, and all of a sudden he can't see! I told him, 'Forget the bullshit. This is the championship. Sit down.'"[56]

Dundee's explanation is found in most of the books I'm familiar with. But there is another explanation that says Liston's corner tried to blind Ali. Muhammad Ali told Thomas Hauser that "a man from Philly" had offered him a bottle of some yellow liquid before his fight with Holmes. A little of that on the glove, and your opponent is temporarily blinded. Later there were also rumors of strange incidents in Liston's other fights. There is no way to know. Peter Fuller, a psychologist, has an entirely different explanation for what happened. In his book *Champions: The Secret Motives in Games and Sports*,[57] he interprets Clay's "blinding" as a displaced fear of castration. In the moment of triumph over an opponent who has been presented as overpowering, Clay actualized an oedipal scenario. Who knows. The facts are, however, that Ali can barely see anything; that among blacks at ringside word spreads like wildfire that his white trainer (Dundee) has blinded Clay; that Dundee uses the same sponge that he wipes Clay down with between rounds to wipe his own eyes, and thereby allays the conspiracy theories; that Clay is yelling "I can't see!" so loud that the referee takes notice, and Dundee shoves the mouthpiece into Clay's mouth to quiet him down; and that he finally shoves Clay into the ring with the words "This is the big one, daddy. Stay away from him. Run!"[58]

At that moment Clay/Ali's entire career hangs in the balance, and in looking back, Ferdie Pacheco, the doctor at ringside, has said: "Angelo was spectacular. He's not one of the best, he's the best cornerman I've ever seen. And what he did between rounds was the best example I can give you of a cornerman seizing a situation and making it right. . . . And if Cassius had been with a corner of amateurs, there would never have been any Muhammad Ali. The fight would have been over. Liston would never have fought him again. And as a member of the Muslims, who were about as popular then as the PLO, Cassius would have sunk from view. . . . Just going out for the fifth round was an incredibly brave thing to do. Liston was considered as destructive as Mike Tyson before Tyson got beat. It was like blinding someone and sending them out to fight Tyson, and Cassius was absolutely brilliant then."[59]

And indeed Cassius Clay fights almost the entire fifth round without being able to see his opponent clearly. Liston hits, Clay goes into a clinch, Liston bangs away at Clay, Clay shoves Liston off, keeping both hands up to protect his head, but Liston doesn't follow through consistently, failing to perceive his chance.[60] All the same, he does connect a few times, hard. Clay changes over to keeping Liston at a distance with his outstretched left arm. After the fight, Liston is supposed to have said that he could have broken Clay's arm, but the reporter who passed on this statement dryly adds that Liston forgot to say why he hadn't done it. In short, Clay succeeds in keeping Liston off him by wildly peppering away at Liston's face, and Liston manages to get through with a truly massive left hook only once. Clay connects just one time in the entire round.

In round six Cassius Clay demonstrates his superiority. He doesn't "dance" but stands flat-footed, lets Liston throw a hesitant jab, and then pummels him with combinations. There's no escape now. Clay advances, Liston retreats, Clay throws hard left jabs, eases back a little, feints, punches, hitting Liston at will. The round is somewhat slower, but that only means the blows land all the harder. And Liston, this tall, strong, somber man—it is obvious now—is afraid of this youngster, who is defeating him here blow by blow, humiliating him for all to see. After the fight, he will say: "That's not the guy I was supposed to fight. That guy could punch!"[61] Liston does not take the ring for the seventh round. Clay climbs up onto the ring post, stretches out an arm in the direction of the press seats: "I told you! I told you! You wouldn't believe me, but I told you!"[62]

Ten years and six months later, Muhammad Ali is standing opposite George Foreman, in an attempt to win the heavyweight title a second time. George Foreman is generally viewed as a second Sonny Liston, or, more precisely, as the man Liston had only appeared to be. Foreman had knocked down both Ken Norton and Joe Frazier within two rounds. People were more cautious this time with their prognoses, but the bookies' odds against Muhammad Ali were at 3 to 1. Before the fight, Archie Moore, the former light-heavyweight champ, who was part of Foreman's camp, was truly worried about Muhammad Ali's health and safety: "Archie Moore, who had his head bowed, found himself thinking that he should pray for Muhammad Ali's safety. Here's what he said: 'I was praying, and in great sincerity, that George wouldn't *kill* Ali. I really felt that was a possibility.'"[63] That quote is from Norman Mailer's book about the fight, and all the hoopla that attended it, in Kinshasa, Zaire. Mailer describes the first seconds after the bell for the first round like this: "The bell! Through a long unheard sigh of collective release, Ali charged across the ring. He looked as big and determined as Foreman, so he held himself, as if *he* possessed the true threat."[64]

The first punch that connects is a hard right to Foreman's forehead: "Ali was not dancing. Rather he was bouncing from side to side looking for an opportunity to attack. So was Foreman. Maybe fifteen seconds went by. Suddenly Ali hit him again. It was again a right hand. Again it was hard. . . . Up and down the press rows, one exclamation was leaping, 'He's hitting him with *rights.*' Ali had not punched with such authority in seven years. Champions do not hit other champions with right-hand leads. Not in the first round. It is the most difficult and dangerous punch. Difficult to deliver and dangerous to oneself. In nearly all positions, the right hand has longer to travel, a foot more at least than the left. Boxers deal with inches and half-inches. In the time it takes a right hand to travel that extra space, alarms are ringing in the opponent, counterattacks are beginning. He will duck under the right and take off your head with a left. So good fighters do not often lead with their right against another good fighter. Not in the first round. They wait. They keep the right hand. It is one's authority, and ready to punish a left which comes too slowly. One throws one's right over a jab; one can block the left hook with a right forearm and chop back a right in return. Classic maxims of boxing. All fight writers know them. Of these principles they take their interpretation. There are good engineers at Indianapolis, but Ali is on his way to the moon. Right-hand leads! My God!"[65] The punch is unconventional for a classic right-hander. But Ali is working for combinations, and that is why he has taken the stance described at the start of the book. The placement of the legs, but not the position of the hands, is that of a man who leads with his left. Ali sees to it that both hands are kept at as nearly the same distance from his opponent as possible. And Ali is no longer holding his hands low, by the way; he isn't quick enough for that anymore. They are now both at head level, but again, not in a classic defensive position but ready for attack. You can tell that from the way he often still dodges Foreman's jabs with his head, instead of parrying them with his fists or arms, and from the way he prefers punching back immediately to taking the detour of a defensive move.

Then comes a combination: right jab, left hook. Ali wanted to make it clear to Foreman from the very start that this fight would go differently from what everyone had imagined; that it would not be a reprise of the Liston fight, at least not in the version of that fight that was lodged in everyone's memory; that he was not going to dance around Foreman and pepper away with left jabs. He wanted to make it clear to Foreman that everything they had taught him, Foreman, in those months of training would be useless trash. The problem that Foreman's trainers and managers had grappled with—"How do you get a fix on Muhammad Ali?"—did not apply for Muhammad Ali. He stood fixed in the center of the ring, and he was the one who attacked. Not with light left jabs, but with powerful right ones. "And then right before the fight, Ali told me he had a plan. He was gonna go out and hit Foreman with a straight right hand as soon as the bell rang. I said, 'No, champ; no! You're gonna dance.' And he told me, 'No, I'm going out and hit Foreman upside his head, so he'll know he's in a fight.'"[66] Archie Moore recalls: "George was the most dangerous puncher of his time. And what I remember most about that fight was, Ali rushed out at the opening bell, showing no fear, and struck George on top of the head. Plans upset; do you know what I mean?"[67]

This first round sees several brilliant combinations from Ali, and Foreman is frustrated in his attempt to punch back. Ali blocks every one of Foreman's attacks, grabs him by the neck with his left, wrestles him down, and blocks his fists until the referee separates them. Ali is a master of this less spectacular technique as well. But in the last third of the round Foreman lands a right uppercut, Ali goes into the clinch, and two full right hooks bang against Ali's head, followed by two to the body, blows of the sort that Foreman was accustomed to ending his fights with in the first round. Ali's eyes go wide, and it appears to be clear to him in that moment what he has to prepare himself, and his body, for. Ali has to absorb two more powerful blows in this round. George Foreman is definitely not ready to be polished off with a few right jabs. He may be irritated by them, but he is not about to have his battle plan upset. And that plan consists of moving in on Ali, fixing him in position against the ropes or wherever, and then pounding away until he falls over. Ali isn't dancing around the ring? All the better, that spares Foreman the trouble of chasing him, and he can start right in with his punches. But for now at any rate, Ali is still eluding Foreman, won't let himself be pushed up against the ropes. He is still too fast, too agile, but he now knows that he will not be able to avoid being hit. Ali is ten years older than he was at the time of the Liston fight, and Foreman is five years younger, and stronger, than he. The demonstration of authority at the start of the first round was good, but it was not a strategy. And while Ali lets Foreman come at him, parrying and countering punches, going into clinches, he tries to find his strategy for this fight.

The second round finds Muhammad Ali busy testing out what George Foreman will do if he lets him do what he wants, and Ali discovers it is always the same thing: drive Ali to the ropes and work him over with heavy left and right sideswipes, trying to batter the cover of his arms away so that he can then land a punch to the gut or the head. Ali lets Foreman do this at various spots around the ring, in one corner, then in the opposite, on the ropes, and now and then he frees himself again with short, hard lefts and jabs at Foreman's head. "I didn't really plan what happened that night. But when a fighter gets in the ring, he has to adjust according to the conditions he faces. Against George, the ring was slow. Dancing all night, my legs would have got tired. And George was following me too close, cutting off the ring. In the first round, I used more energy staying away from him than he used chasing me. I was tireder than I should have been with fourteen rounds to go. . . . So starting in the second round, I gave George what he thought he wanted. And he hit hard."[68]

At the start of the third round, Ali serves Foreman a combination of three punches, but then goes to the ropes—more as a withdrawal than because he was actually being forced to retreat there. Ali has found his style for the fight, and it is the exact opposite of what had been expected, the opposite of what had made Ali famous in the eyes of most of his admirers. Let us compare the strategies of the two boxers. What George Foreman is looking for is "the one big punch"; it needn't be the first punch, or the second, it can be the seventy-eighth, but come it must. Which is why George Foreman doesn't build combinations, doesn't throw his punches in clusters, but in sequence, one-two-one-two. In order to achieve the greatest possible effect from each punch, he needs to be stationary, and his opponent has to be a fixed target. His every move in the ring serves to bring about that situation. The ultimate goal is a victory with his opponent on the mat—dominance achieved by ending the fight, dominance *after* the fight. Muhammad Ali, on the other hand, is looking for combinations of punches, dominance in a given fight *situation*. A fighter has to precipitate such a situation, but that is part of a dynamic not so clearly defined as the static situation of a solid punch. Ali therefore needs a second kind of dominance, over the *flow* of movement in the ring. George Foreman is attempting to achieve a certain static situation that is to his advantage, while Ali is trying to dominate a dynamic process. He was successful at it in the fight against Liston. Clay had used Liston's attempts to chase him to bring about situations in which he could land combinations to Liston's head, ultimately forcing him to give up. He had achieved something similar in a

good many other fights. But not in the bouts against
Norton and Frazier, at least not convincingly. How
was he to succeed at it now in Foreman's case? Like
this: "I gave George what he thought he wanted." Ali
let George Foreman do what he planned to do, and
adjusted his own moves accordingly. Muhammad Ali
was like a speaker in a debate who has been slipped
his opponent's crib sheet and so knows moment by
moment what his adversary is going to say next. The
site Muhammad Ali chose for his combination punches
was the ropes, the very place to which George Foreman would try to drive him. As for the point in time—
it remained to be seen how long it would take before
the exertion of battering away at another human being
(who won't do what all those blows are supposed to
make him do, that is, fall down), before Muhammad
Ali's own blows to Foreman's head, the heat of the
Zairean night, and, finally, the frustration associated
with all of that would bring George Foreman to a state
where one of those combinations would have to result
in a knockout. Such a strategy presumes an even larger
measure of physical sacrifice, one is tempted to say, of
masochism, than is normal in the sport of boxing.
Above all, however, five senses are challenged with a
paradoxical task. First, they must be willing to take the
most dreadful blows, but second, they can never
slacken in attentiveness, for only then will the blows
lead to unconsciousness. And meanwhile Ali has to be
monitoring the state of his opponent as carefully as if
he were one of Foreman's own corner men.

With the start of the third round, Ali has decided
to take on all these tasks. Dismay erupts both in his

corner and among the spectators. "Get out of the corner! Get off the ropes! Move, Ali! Dance!" But Ali doesn't dance, he leans way back into the ropes, holds his fists up to his face, his forearms clasped tight to cover his head, chest, solar plexus, and stomach, and when the opportunity allows—that is, when the not yet exhausted but certainly thoroughly enraged Foreman allows—he punches viciously from this position, hard blows to Foreman's face. The punches he himself has to absorb rack his body—left, right, jabs, hooks, and not all of them land in the cover, several get through to the gut, to the head, get past the protecting fists to the chin, and those watching ask helplessly what is going on here, why would anyone let that be done to him? Is Ali washed up? Where is "the old Ali," "the young Clay"? They are watching him. He is busy beating George Foreman.

"Muhammad amazed me; I'll admit it. He outthought me; he outfought me. That night, he was just the better man in the ring. Before the fight, I thought I'd knock him out easy. One round, two rounds. I was very confident. And what I remember most about the fight was, I went out and hit Muhammad with the hardest shot to the body I ever delivered to any opponent. Anybody else in the world would have crumbled. Muhammad cringed; I could see it hurt. And then he looked at me; he had that look in his eyes, like he was saying I'm not gonna let you hurt me. And to be honest, that's the main thing I remember about the fight. Everything else happened too quick. I got burned out. . . . You see, Muhammad's antennas were built to look out for big punches. And with the style I had, my height, and my tendency to throw big punches—no matter how hard I hit, Muhammad had the instinct to get ready for each punch, ride it through, and be waiting for the next one. I was the aggressor; there was no doubt about that. I was throwing the most punches, but I knew that in some way I was losing. In fact, I remember thinking during the fight, hey, this guy wasn't champion before because someone bought the title for him. He's good."[69]

A brief scene at the beginning of round four anticipates the end of the fight. Ali backs off from Foreman into the corner, both fighters feint. Then comes Foreman's left jab, once, twice, he is holding his right very low in preparation for the upward thrust of a hook. Suddenly Ali throws a right cross over Foreman's outstretched left, lands a left jab, followed by a right. The blows come so quickly, one after the other, that it takes slow motion to make out the sequence. And they do the job. For a moment Foreman looks as if he has been hurt. His face, too, shows the marks of Ali's punches. The rest of the round, however, takes on a now familiar look: Muhammad Ali lying sprawled on the ropes; George Foreman, his hands stretched out in front of him, trying to throw Ali off-balance with big punches. Ali just keeps blocking Foreman and shoving him into the middle of the ring, then he untangles himself and changes to another corner. And in between, again and again, the left and right jabs to Foreman's face. Shortly before the bell, Foreman lands a hard left hook.

"Foreman came out in the fifth," Mailer writes, "with the conviction that if force had not prevailed against Ali up to now, more force was the answer."[70] And indeed all the force he had thrown against Ali in previous rounds was nothing compared to what he showed now. Foreman apparently sensed that his energies were beginning to ebb, and so had decided to finish Ali off in this fifth round. To the spectators it looked as if he might very possibly succeed. Ali stood at the ropes, leaning way back, his head protected by his double cover, and was literally tossed back and forth by Foreman's blows. Mailer describes it like this: "Foreman kept flashing his muscles up out of that cup of desperation boiling in all determination, punches that came toward the end of what may have been as many as forty or fifty in a minute, any one strong enough to send water from the spine to the knees."[71] No one would have been surprised if Ali's resistance had been broken by the end of this round. The fact is that at the end of round five Ali puts together one of the best offenses of the entire bout. First he throws a left jab, a right cross, another left and a right, almost like a test, as if probing Foreman's reaction, then he lets himself fall back into the ropes. Foreman attacks, but without focus, and from the ropes Ali throws a left and a right, tries to twist out of the ropes and past Foreman, Foreman steps back, but so does Ali, Foreman apparently thinks it's up to him to march forward again, but now Ali goes on the attack, four powerful hits totally confound Foreman's defense, he is driven back, Ali takes a step back, Foreman advances and meets two more punches, then another two, one of them a crashing right to Foreman's jaw, thrown with no less power than any of Foreman's blows in the round. Mailer quotes one of the commentators at ringside. "I really don't believe it. I thought he was hurt. I thought his body was hurt. He came back. He hit Foreman with everything."[72]

Not only had Ali hit Foreman harder, presumably, than he had ever been hit by any boxer in his career, but above all, he, Foreman, had also hit Ali harder than he had ever hit any boxer before—by the end of the round the psychological effect on Foreman must have been devastating. The next two rounds, especially compared to the fifth, are rather boring. Foreman can find no other solution than the neurotic's "more of the same," and round five has used up a lot of his energy reserves. Ali now knew that his strategy was successful, he had survived the worst, he only had to avoid mistakes and wait for Foreman's exhaustion and dwindling concentration to reach levels needed for a knockout. To be sure, the imponderable factor in the equation was the fact that Ali's energies were ebbing, too. The fifth round had demanded his utmost. No wonder, then, that the next two rounds were considerably less dramatic than those before them. For almost the entire bout, by the way, Muhammad Ali talked to George Foreman. What he said has not been handed down, but judging from the look on his face at the start of round six, they were words full of mockery and disdain. But at the end of round seven, Foreman can still deliver a mighty blow to Ali's stomach and land an uppercut to his chin. "This man, Muhammad Ali, is *unreal,*" says one of the commentators.

Round eight—Muhammad Ali ends the fight. Before the bell, there is a little joke. In the United States, young women usually walk across the ring carrying signs with the number of the next round. In Kinshasa the signs are little cloths, like oversize handkerchiefs, and the woman carrying the notice for round eight holds her cloth wrong, so that the sign reads "∞" (infinity).

Ali begins the round with three fierce lefts to Foreman's head, one after the other, with short breaks in between. Foreman throws a hook that is way off the mark, but its inertia tugs him on past Ali, and Foreman almost falls over the ropes. Then the battle continues as in the two rounds before. For another thirty seconds. Ali is standing in the corner again, throws a short combination, Foreman attacks slowly, takes a hit, misses with a left hook, once again the inertia pulls him past Ali, he absorbs a blow, Ali twists out of the corner, Foreman is on the ropes, Ali lands a right, Foreman's arms move uncoordinatedly, he almost reels into Ali, a right hook, a devastating left hook, Foreman's head is whipped around, a right jab to the middle of the face, Foreman begins to fall, he falls slowly, his arms trying to grab the air, past Ali, who holds his attack position as he watches the motion. It takes Foreman two full seconds to fall, then he is lying on the canvas and is counted out. "That was no phantom-punch! That was no phantom-punch! And he is down and out!" Muhammad Ali has regained his title. "After the fight, for a while I was bitter. . . . And then, finally, I realized I'd lost to a great champion; probably the greatest of all time . . . [A]nd now I'm just proud to be part of the Ali legend. If people mention my name with his from time to time, that's enough for me. That, and I hope Muhammad likes me, because I like him. I like him a lot."[73]

MANILA, XIII AND XIV

R ound thirteen. Both boxers in the center of the ring, a light exchange of punches. Ali goes to the ropes briefly, then shoves Frazier back to the center of the ring. Ali is moving on his toes, holding his fists and forearms almost relaxed at waist level. Frazier advances, ducks, but doesn't punch, he's readying a left hook—a hard right to Frazier's head, Frazier buckles forward. Ali almost falls over him, shoves him away, Frazier advances again, ducks, a left hook by Ali misses, Frazier punches, one, two, three times, then the two exhausted boxers embrace, but Ali shoves the heavier Joe Frazier off him once more. Ali is now standing erect with one leg forward, his weight resting on the other, arms dangling, Frazier comes at him, throwing his gloves up to his face defensively. Ali strikes, takes a few steps past Frazier, throws a left that Frazier deflects, then connects with a right. Frazier's mouthpiece flies off in a high arc. Another right, a left, a right. Ali is on his toes, he isn't dancing, but he is punching as he moves.

You can't lie to a machine, can't make a fool of it, José Torres had written, and Frazier was a fighting machine. Frazier was not waiting to land a decisive "big punch"; he succeeded with that only occasionally, had succeeded with it against Ali in New York. Frazier's strategy was to wear Muhammad Ali down, drain him, and it is one thing if, like Foreman, you flail away in vain at an opponent, but quite another if those blows are part of what you are out to accomplish. For Foreman, every punch that didn't knock Ali down was a defeat; for Frazier every punch that connected with Ali's body was a piece of victory. Ali had to prove to Foreman that he would never be able to land the punch that he was hoping for; that he, Ali, would absorb anything Foreman had to dish out to him, and at the end still be able to strike Foreman with hard, precise blows. Ali's combinations had not been able to conquer Frazier in their first fight; in the second they had garnered him more points—that had been all. Muhammad Ali had never been able to dominate Joe Frazier. If he wanted to do it now in the few rounds still left, a matter of less than nine minutes, he would have to change the pattern of movement that had characterized the previous twenty-four rounds of Muhammad Ali vs. Joe Frazier. He had to chase Frazier. Ali could do it because Frazier was exhausted. But Ali had to do it at a point when he himself was exhausted, certainly more fatigued, more battered than he had been in Zaire, than he had ever been in his life.

Ali lands a right jab, a left hook. Frazier misses a punch, Ali misses a punch. Ali is in the corner, Frazier falls almost on top of him, Ali pulls him closer, and Frazier almost topples over the ropes. The referee separates them. Ali moves at Frazier, Frazier raises his hands, Ali lands a right. Left, right, left, a right hook is wide of the mark, a left connects. Another left hook, Frazier seeks the protection of a clinch, the referee separates them. Ali pushes Frazier's fists to the side, connects, connects with his left, his right—clinch, the referee separates them.

Near Ali, in the ropes—that had been Frazier's attack position in past rounds, and now he seeks refuge there himself. The referee separates them. A right jab, a left, another right. Frazier reels. A left connects, a right goes astray, Frazier tries a hook again, steps into Ali's counterpunch. Ali is not punching uninterruptedly. He has to catch his breath, mobilize energy from somewhere for each blow. He punches, with speed and power, always in combinations of two, three, sometimes four blows. He keeps pushing Frazier back upright, who tries to escape in the clinch. Bell.

Round fourteen. At first it looks as if Ali cannot finish what he started in the last two rounds, but then, with the round half over, the destruction of Joe Frazier begins anew. Ali hits Frazier at will. A minute left in the round. A right hook, a left, a right jab, a left hook, a left jab, a wide swing for a left hook, Frazier backs away. Ali follows him, left jab, right, Ali moves past Frazier, lands a right, then a left, and is now on the other side of the ring—he has descended upon Frazier like a thunderstorm. And the rest of the round is the same. Ali lands powerful blows to Frazier's head again and again, and Joe Frazier is no longer in a position to parry. At times he tries to counter, but his punches miss by a mile. Another forty seconds. Ali throws a right, Frazier dodges to one side, both boxers turn, Ali lands a left, then a right jab directly to Frazier's face. Another left. Frazier strikes back with a left, Ali blocks with a right cross, hitting Frazier squarely. Then both boxers are worn out, the referee separates them, Frazier tries a left hook, missing Ali by a foot at least, he stumbles past Ali. Frazier can no longer get a clear look at Ali, his eyes are swollen shut. He has had to absorb another twelve powerful blows to the head in this round. Joe Frazier does not appear for round fifteen. His trainer, Eddie Futch, stops the fight. Frazier can scarcely see anything now, his left eye is swollen shut, and he can no longer see Ali's right hand coming.

When the bell for round fifteen sounds, Muhammad Ali gets up for the last round. But then he realizes the fight is over. He lifts one arm, then collapses. When he comes to again, he speaks into a microphone shoved into his face: "I want to retire, this is too painful, this is too much work."

"In Manila I threw him punches, they'd of knocked a building over. And he took 'em. He took 'em, and he came back, and I got to respect that part of the man. He was a fighter. He shook me in Manila; he won."

"I don't think that two big men have ever fought like me and Joe Frazier. One fight, maybe. But three times; we were the only ones. Of all the men I fought in boxing, Sonny Liston was the scariest; George Foreman was the most powerful; Floyd Patterson was the most skilled as a boxer. But my roughest and toughest was Joe Frazier. He brought out the best in me, and the best we fought was in Manila. That fight I could feel something happening to me. Something different from what I'd felt before."[74]

After the fight, Ali repeated what he had said in the pause before round twelve. "Later, he said that fight was the closest thing to death he knew of. And he was right."[75]

EPILOGUE

And so what drove us to sit in front of the TV late that night was not some infatuation with the primal—which, even though I tried to dismiss it initially with a bit of affectation, surely is an inescapable part of watching brawls and indeed leaves us gaping indiscriminately at all brawlers—no, it was Muhammad Ali there on the screen. Boxers who seem to dissolve into the archaic—the Mike Tysons of all weight divisions—are good only for a regressive kick, and for answering that question we all easily forget again in a moment: Who is the current reigning champ?

Does that then imply that the fascination exerted by Muhammad Ali's style is in fact perfectly civilized? The triumph of a well-rounded personality over the archaic element, something like Theseus vs. the Minotaur? No, I think we have to rule out that possibility as well. For ultimately, the Listons, Foremans, Fraziers, and Tysons are, if anything, men with what is called personality, precisely because they have a clearer, more recognizable, more definable style than does Muhammad Ali, who, to use the phrase Ernst Bloch applied to the compositional style of Igor Stravinsky, is "the mask that can always be something different."

I believe the fascination that emanated from Muhammad Ali had more to do with our watching a human type that we basically do not know at all, which for now is intimated only in its first traits, but to which the future probably belongs. To explain this, I must first indulge in a bit of anthropological speculation.

No matter what kind of community human beings may live in, they must always do one thing: they must reconcile the call of instinct with the claims made upon them by their particular community—the "demands of culture," to use Freud's term. *One* way to do this is to develop and cultivate individuality. To be an individual means to bear within one's own breast, so to speak, the contradictions of instinctual and cultural demands. That effort generally ends up leading to various neuroses—which, however, do not imply that the attempt has failed, but rather are merely side effects of the attempt, for it seldom or never succeeds without some difficulties. This attempt to reconcile instinctual and cultural demands likewise results in the formation of an individual biography, individual character traits, and so forth. What we call a person's character is in fact the result of the psychological fine-tuning that emerges out of the personal psychological crises that are inevitable when instinctual and cultural demands are brought into what is always a precarious balance.

Now, as I noted, individuality is only one possible way for a person to adjust to living in a social unit— there are others. Since we are accustomed to placing such a high value on our style of life as individuals— and hidden in our self-admiration is a bit of compensation for our own normal neurotic miseries—we usually imply some disparagement when we say that other people possess no real individuality. And indeed we have no good word for describing individual human beings who lack real individuality. I shall therefore— quite inadmissibly, to be sure—expand the concept of individuality and take it as my synonym for the more general notion of the "individual human being." But that means we need the services of an adjective to define the classic concept of "individuality"—and I suggest that it be the word "balanced."

In various eras in history the balanced individual has been the dominant type. Historically, he or she first came into view in *The Odyssey,* but achieved a kind of real self-understanding only somewhat later. In the Greek tragedies we first see him highlighted against an archaic background in the figure of Orestes, first experience her moral triumph in *Antigone,* and first witness how such an individual comes to realize his own peril

in *The Bacchae*. Much later, in the sixteenth and sev-
enteenth centuries, we watch the balanced individual
rediscover himself—we can even designate fairly
precisely a point in space and time: around 1588 at
Château Montaigne, when Michel de Montaigne com-
pleted the heart of his essays. Of course we can also
find balanced individuals during that long stretch
between the end of antiquity and modernity's begin-
nings in the Renaissance—but such people were not
the predominant type. A detailed answer to the question of "Why?" would more than burst the framework
of this little speculation, and so in that regard, just one
laconic remark: It did not always pay to be a balanced
individual—Abelard's letters to Héloïse can also be
read from that viewpoint. Or put the other way around:
from some point in history on, certain social rewards
accrued to the effort of being a balanced individual. A
balanced individual displays certain virtues—the ability to delay instinctual drives, to specialize one's labor,
a capacity for abstraction, prudence, foresight, frugal-
ity, self-imposed discipline. And there came a time
when those virtues were in demand and brought success. The triumph of capitalist European civilization
and the ascendancy of balanced individuality go hand
in hand. The virtues of the balanced individual are the
specific virtues of modernity. With them, one can build
a grand enterprise, be it a factory or a hospital, plan the
logistics of a war, envision a welfare state, write a novel
or run a concentration camp.

Balanced individuality was learned over the course of
history, and it must be learned anew in each individual

case. Once learned, however, life lived as a balanced individual is anything but secure, both on a social and an individual level. Societies as well as individuals can regress to a pre-balanced state. This occurs when the burdens of holding the demands of instinct and culture in balance become too great, or when it simply no longer pays to do so—or when regression does pay. In that case people who have previously been balanced individuals are able to abandon their internal governing mechanism en masse, replacing it with a real or imagined führer and surrendering to him. "Command, and we follow!" they cry—and also discard a piece of personality that differentiated them from others. The führer's will replaces personal conscience.

The word "regression" implies that this is a step back into an earlier stage. And that is true, at least to the extent that individuals left that earlier stage behind in order to become balanced individuals. (And we can say with some certainty that the same thing is true in a historical sense.) But when we use the term "earlier stage," we ought not to imagine a stage that knew nothing of the problem of mediating the demands of instinct and culture—the problem was simply solved differently then. Through ritual. In societies where the balanced individual predominates, each separate person has to make sure that the ways in which his or her instincts get gratified are socially acceptable. If they are not, punishment follows, and the person is often removed from all social interaction—is imprisoned, even killed. In the "previous stage" it was society itself that made sure its members did not endanger it. It did so either by providing acceptable behaviors in which aggression and sexual wishes were gratified under controlled conditions or by supplying people with an adequate substitute for the lack of such gratification. Here, too, there are punishments, but they have other rules and a different meaning. Where the reconciliation of instinctual and cultural demands is not a matter of the individual, but of his society, the individual is much more a part of that society. I suggest we call such a person the "associated" individual. Both as an individual and as a member of society, the balanced individual always carries the associated individual inside him, so to speak—that is, he can always regress to that stage. We can also observe the presence of that stage in the continued existence of religions, great and small, in team sports, in neuroses and their boon companions: flaws, tics, and obsessive behaviors—which, as Freud repeatedly pointed out, have a kinship with the rituals of primitive societies.

The next question is this: Is the balanced individual, compared to the associated, history's final word, so to speak? Is he or she still the more advanced type in our own time? I think the answer must be no. In fact, we can all observe that over the course of this century it has proved less and less rewarding to cultivate the virtues of a balanced individual and at the same time to bear all the consequent sufferings and annoyances. What is at work here appears to be the interaction of two tendencies whose origins are not directly related. First, there is the increasing complexity of all social processes—what Norbert Elias has called the "society of long paths." In such a society the balanced individual is no longer reimbursed for his expenses, so to speak. His specific achievement—his daily coping with having renounced his instinctual drives, only to suffer, like Goethe's Torquato Tasso, until life's end—is no longer honored by society. The individual is able to count fewer and fewer social processes as his or her "personal achievement."

The second of these two interacting tendencies seeks to destroy civilization. The self-image of modern civilization was first outlined in Thomas Hobbes's metaphor of the Leviathan. Three centuries later, in *Civilization and Its Discontents,* Sigmund Freud solidified that image in his theory of instincts. According to Freud, the community, the state, disarms the individual and monopolizes power. The individual then transforms his own aggressive tendencies into conscience and guilt feelings. On the basis of such a self-image, civilization regards cruelty, the excessive use of force, as antithetical to itself. The first great shock to civilization's self-image was World War I. Auschwitz was its refutation. At Auschwitz, a genocide lacking all civilized rationality was carried out under the aegis of every sort of civilized virtue (prudence, lack of passion, fulfillment of duty). Together with other great crimes of the century, Auschwitz, as the most bizarre and horrible example,[76] destroyed the basic certainty that was one of the chief promises of civilization. That same certainty had sustained the effort required to form a balanced individual.

In his analysis of reports from German concentration camps,[77] Leo Löwenthal has pointed out that the terror in the camps led to the "fragmentation" of individuals subjected to it, turning their actions into a sequence of conditioned reflexes. Walter Benjamin has analyzed the difficulty that the "modern" human being has in perceiving what happens to him as "experience"—events in his life "befall" him like a series of shocks. The upshot of Norbert Elias's analysis of the society of long paths is that human beings are less and less capable of gaining an overview of what constitutes their actions, are no longer able to recognize a beginning or an end, so that a goal and success in life become empty categories. It would be absurd to claim that all this is cut from the same cloth. Worlds separate the horrors of a concentration camp from the everyday frustrations of the ordinary person. I would be inappropriately applying the sort of outdated historical metaphysics whose very demise appears to have gone hand in hand with the death of the balanced individual, if I were to claim that all these things are manifestations of one and the same historical trend. Just the opposite is the case. Social changes, historical events, the inevitability of technological progress, and the contingency of political events have worked together to produce what only appears to us to be a homogeneous process: the destruction of the balanced individual.

Regression to a "preindividual" condition, or, to stick with my own terminology, to the associated individual, is *one* of the possible answers to the crisis faced by the balanced individual. In some countries political reality has been reorganized as little more than gang warfare—which seems to indicate that the associated individual may be well on its way to experiencing a renaissance. But let us not deceive ourselves. The member of a band of murderers in Serbia, Croatia, or wherever ultimately has no more in common with a tribal warrior than does a member of a street gang in Frankfurt or Los Angeles. And the feat of coping with the demands of our social and technological institutions—which themselves are rapidly growing ever more complex—is not going to be accomplished by some sort of regression. As a rule, each of us moves through modern society as a single human being within the mass, but not as an associated individual dissolving into it. The person who has adjusted to the society of long paths is someone I would like to call a "dissociated" individual. The dissociated individual does not plunge into archaic ecstasies but instead comes equipped with a vast repertoire of differentiated abilities. Anyone who has ever attempted to explain to an adult who has never been to an airport everything you must do in order to finally take your seat in a flying machine has some notion of the capacities each modern individual has at his or her disposal. The savage who can perceive the track of a gazelle's hoof on even the hardest stone is an overspecialized idiot in comparison with a modern-day human being. What vast flexibility is needed for each of us to cope with arenas of action that no one truly comprehends, and all of this is accomplished within a great variety of institutions whose meaning and function necessarily remain more or less baffling. The life of the dissociated individual is (not completely, but for the most part) a sequence of conditioned reflexes—not of learned rituals but of minuscule acquired reactions, each of them contingent on a given situation.

It may well be that such an individual somehow simply dissolves into all these reactions. In that case the task of mediating instinctual and cultural demands would again fall to the collective. We are familiar with only one way to perform this task: by regression into ritual. The sociological catchwords here are "repressive desublimation" and "thrill-seeking society." But the dissociated individual can no more be defined by these two extreme forms—the "cog in the machine" and the reflex killer (although the two types would appear to become one in front of some video games)— then the balanced type can be characterized by just *one* kind of neurosis. We are standing at the threshold and do not yet have an overview of things. It may also turn out that both the need and a capacity for such an overview will vanish as the dissociated individual becomes a universal type. But the determinative factor for all varieties of the dissociated individual is that none of them form what, in the case of the balanced individual, is called an "identity." The dissociated individual has no "core" from which it understands itself. It skates on the surface, so to speak, among various identities. That statement is, of course, only a makeshift construction, since it presumes an "it" that, although somehow masked, always remains fundamentally the same. But that is not what I mean. The primal image of the dissociated individual is Proteus, the Greek sea god who is eternally transforming himself. One of the most profound allegories in literary history is to be found in the second part of *Faust,* where Goethe unites the mythological Proteus with his homunculus, an artificial man created in a retort.

The psychotic, for example, can also exhibit such Proteus-like traits, and in the psychotic we can recognize one of the embodiments of the modern (perhaps postmodern) dissociated individual. He is no longer the exception that arises when the attempt to form a balanced individual miscarries, but an exceptional case of normality. We must, of course, also include in this same category the so-called multiple personality, of which psychiatry and psychology are becoming increasingly aware. In these cases many, sometimes dozens of different identities and characters (each with no knowledge of the others) are united—or perhaps not united, but simply coexist—while the multiple personality bounds here and there among them. Given his Proteus-like quality, then, the dissociated individual does not stand in total opposition to the classic balanced individual. One of his identities can easily be the classic balanced individual—Woody Allen's *Zelig* is a precise case study of the type.

Each of the three types of individuality—the associated, the balanced, and the dissociated—has both a predominant variation and something that I would like to call its "antitype." In the case of the associated individual, these two literally stand face-to-face: the participant in the ritual and its leader. The group joined in ritual requires someone who stands outside it and sees to it that everything proceeds correctly. That person is the shaman, the priest-king, the grand inquisitor. He is part of the ritual, since he is likewise subject to it, and yet he is not part of it, either, since he cannot dissolve into it. He must also develop the traits of the balanced individual, because the ritual depends on him in a very different sense than it depends on all the others and because the ritual cannot entirely do for him what it does for the others. Historically we can observe the formation of balanced individuality in personalities like those of the Aztec king Montezuma or the inquisitor Bernard Gui.

The predominant variety of the balanced individual is the person who is well adjusted to his society. This can be the respectable citizen and bureaucrat or the creative entrepreneur or politician. It can certainly also be the sort of person who shows a certain wisdom in weighing both his own personal commitment and his insight into what society is able to provide, someone who demonstrates the achievement of balance as the high art of living—"Follow me and don't break your neck!" I mean the "Goethe" type. The antitype of both the respectable citizen and the Goethe type is the eccentric. The eccentric opposes the demands of the collective, demonstratively disdains the feat of achieving balance, loathes the Goethe type, and, if he's lucky, is called "Byronic." In terms of our theoretical system, the task he performs by his opposition is to make the limits against which he rebels visible, thereby helping others not to overstep them by mistake.

Just as the antitype of the associated individual, the leader of the cult, already merges into the realm of the

balanced individual, the dissociated individual likewise manifests itself in the balanced individual's cultural domain. Here the antitype to what will perhaps
one day be the predominant variety explicitly rejects
the role of the eccentric that the normal world would
like to ascribe to him. We are speaking of the megalomaniac. Like the eccentric, he despises the normal
variants of his type, but unlike the eccentric, who
loathes collective *norms* above all else, the megalomaniac's antipathy is directed at both the collective and
the people who represent it. He hates both the "aver-
age man" and the "deindividualized" bundle of conditioned reflexes. The megalomaniac is often a psychotic
with delusions of grandeur, and only in the rarest cases
is he a megalomaniac by rights. In that case—to use
examples from the world of twentieth-century German
thought and literature—his name is Karl Kraus,
Theodor W. Adorno, or Arno Schmidt. Each of them
would have considered it despicable to knuckle under
to normality by being its eccentric exception. Like the
psychotic, who makes his own megalomania plausible
to himself by believing he is Napoleon, the megalomaniac who is truly a genius often acts in the name of
traditions he pretends to serve and for which he pretends to speak. As a rule, however, his relationship to
these traditions is problematic and broken. Though he
is very easily mistaken on the outside for a traditional
bourgeois citizen, above all else he loathes being one
himself. If he is a writer, he typically makes nervous
use of the first person singular—from totally avoiding it
(Adorno) to a virtual inflationary use of it (Schmidt). In

both cases, however, the use of the word "I" is a mask put on to create a recognizable self. The gesture always fails; at times it is even intended to fail.

End of anthropological speculation. Perhaps my readers have guessed what I have been driving at. I believe that Muhammad Ali is a cross between the Proteus-like dissociated individual and its antitype. This applies to his behavior both in and out of the boxing ring. But whereas the "public" Muhammad Ali presented great difficulties to those who wanted to "capture" him,[78] it has always been assumed that it is much easier to describe his boxing style—leading to the familiar failure to recognize what constituted it. Muhammad Ali the person, Muhammad Ali the boxer, can be understood only if one understands the connection between the *dissociated individual* and the *megalomaniac,* or, put another way, between *variability* and *dominance.* And since he was a boxer, one must understand him on the basis of his boxing style—the rest follows on its own.

And then the fascination that Muhammad Ali's image has exerted and still exerts on so many people becomes clear as well. It cannot be separated from the constitutional makeup of those same people. For they, for we, are all transitional types who enjoyed their anticipated future as science fiction in the form of a fifteen-round boxing match—taking greater relish in the destruction of who-they-no-longer-were in the form of Liston, Foreman, and Frazier than in the triumph of what-they-are-not-yet: Proteus as *homo novus* and ruler of worlds.

Appendix

Overview of Fights[79]

11/30/56	Chicago	Floyd Patterson–Archie Moore	W	5 KO*
5/1/59	Indianapolis	Floyd Patterson–Brian London	W	11 KO
6/26/59	New York	Floyd Patterson–I. Johansson	L	3 KO
6/20/60	New York	Floyd Patterson–I. Johansson	W	5 KO
10/29/60	Louisville	Cassius Clay–Tunney Hunsaker	W	6 pts
12/27/60	Miami Beach	Cassius Clay–Herb Siler	W	4 KO
1/17/61	Miami Beach	Cassius Clay–Tony Esperti	W	3 KO
2/7/61	Miami Beach	Cassius Clay–Jim Robinson	W	1 KO
2/21/61	Miami Beach	Cassius Clay–Donnie Fleeman	W	7 KO
3/13/61	Miami Beach	Floyd Patterson–I. Johansson	W	6 KO
4/19/61	Louisville	Cassius Clay–Lamar Clark	W	2 KO
6/26/61	Las Vegas	Cassius Clay–Duke Sabedong	W	10 pts
7/22/61	Louisville	Cassius Clay–Alonzo Johnson	W	10 pts
10/7/61	Louisville	Cassius Clay–Alex Miteff	W	6 KO
11/29/61	Louisville	Cassius Clay–Willie Besmanoff	W	7 KO
2/11/62	New York	Cassius Clay–Sonny Banks	W	4 KO
2/28/62	Miami Beach	Cassius Clay–Don Warner	W	4 KO
4/23/62	Los Angeles	Cassius Clay–George Logan	W	4 KO
5/19/62	New York	Cassius Clay–Billy Daniels	W	7 KO
7/20/62	Los Angeles	Cassius Clay–Alejandro Lavorante	W	5 KO
9/25/62	Chicago	Floyd Patterson–Sonny Liston	L	1 KO
11/15/62	Los Angeles	Cassius Clay–Archie Moore	W	4 KO
1/24/63	Pittsburgh	Cassius Clay–Charlie Powell	W	3 KO

*W = won; L = lost; KO = knockout; pts = points. The figures in the final column represent the number of rounds fought.

3/13/63	New York	Cassius Clay–Doug Jones	W	10 pts
6/18/63	London	Cassius Clay–Henry Cooper	W	5 KO
2/25/64	Miami Beach	Cassius Clay–Sonny Liston	W	7 KO
3/5/65	Chicago	Ernie Terrell–Eddie Machen	W	15 pts
5/25/65	Lewiston, Maine	Muhammad Ali–Sonny Liston	W	1 KO
11/1/65	Toronto	Ernie Terrell–George Chuvalo	W	15 pts
11/22/65	Las Vegas	Muhammad Ali–Floyd Patterson	W	12 KO
3/29/66	Toronto	Muhammad Ali–George Chuvalo	W	15 pts
5/21/66	London	Muhammad Ali–Henry Cooper	W	6 KO
6/28/66	Houston	Ernie Terrell–Doug Jones	W	15 pts
8/6/66	London	Muhammad Ali–Brian London	W	3 KO
9/10/66	Frankfurt	Muhammad Ali–Karl Mildenberger	W	12 KO
11/14/66	Houston	Muhammad Ali–Cleveland Williams	W	3 KO
2/6/67	Houston	Muhammad Ali–Ernie Terrell	W	15 pts
3/22/67	New York	Muhammad Ali–Zora Folley	W	7 KO
4/27/68	Oakland	Jimmy Ellis–Jerry Quarry	W	15 pts
9/14/68	Stockholm	Jimmy Ellis–Floyd Patterson	W	15 pts
12/10/68	Philadelphia	Joe Frazier–Oscar Bonavena	W	15 pts
6/23/69	New York	Joe Frazier–Jerry Quarry	W	7 KO
2/16/70	New York	Joe Frazier–Jimmy Ellis	W	5 KO
10/26/70	Atlanta	Muhammad Ali–Jerry Quarry	W	3 KO
11/18/70	Detroit	Joe Frazier–Bob Foster	W	2 KO
12/7/70	New York	Muhammad Ali–Oscar Bonavena	W	15 KO
3/8/71	New York	Muhammad Ali–Joe Frazier	L	15 pts
7/26/71	Houston	Muhammad Ali–Jimmy Ellis	W	12 KO
11/17/71	Houston	Muhammad Ali–Buster Mathis	W	12 pts
12/26/71	Zurich	Muhammad Ali–Jürgen Blin	W	7 KO
4/1/72	Tokyo	Muhammad Ali–Mac Foster	W	15 pts
5/1/72	Vancouver	Muhammad Ali–George Chuvalo	W	12 pts
6/27/72	Las Vegas	Muhammad Ali–Jerry Quarry	W	7 KO
7/19/72	Dublin	Muhammad Ali–Al Lewis	W	11 KO
9/20/72	New York	Muhammad Ali–Floyd Patterson	W	7 KO
11/21/72	Stateline, Nevada	Muhammad Ali–Bob Foster	W	8 KO
1/22/73	Kingston, Jamaica	Joe Frazier–George Foreman	L	2 KO
2/14/73	Las Vegas	Muhammad Ali–Joe Bugner	W	12 pts

3/31/73	San Diego	Muhammad Ali–Ken Norton	L	12 pts
9/10/73	Los Angeles	Muhammad Ali–Ken Norton	W	12 pts
10/21/73	Djakarta	Muhammad Ali–Rudi Lubbers	W	12 pts
3/26/74	Caracas	George Foreman–Ken Norton	W	2 KO
1/28/74	New York	Muhammad Ali–Joe Frazier	W	12 pts
10/30/74	Kinshasa	Muhammad Ali–George Foreman	W	8 KO
3/24/75	Cleveland	Muhammad Ali–Chuck Wepner	W	15 KO
5/16/75	Las Vegas	Muhammad Ali–Ron Lyle	W	11 KO
6/30/75	Malaysia	Muhammad Ali–Joe Bugner	W	15 pts
10/1/75	Manila	Muhammad Ali–Joe Frazier	W	14 KO
2/20/76	San Juan	Muhammad Ali–J.-P. Coopman	W	5 KO
4/30/76	Landover, Maryland	Muhammad Ali–Jimmy Young	W	15 pts
5/24/76	Munich	Muhammad Ali–Richard Dunn	W	5 KO
9/28/76	New York	Muhammad Ali–Ken Norton	W	15 KO
5/16/77	Landover, Maryland	Muhammad Ali–Alfredo Evangelista	W	15 pts
9/29/77	New York	Muhammad Ali–Earnie Shavers	W	15 pts
2/15/78	Las Vegas	Muhammad Ali–Leon Spinks	L	15 pts
6/10/78	Las Vegas	Ken Norton–Larry Holmes	L	15 pts
9/15/78	New Orleans	Muhammad Ali–Leon Spinks	W	15 pts
11/10/78	Las Vegas	Larry Holmes–Alfredo Evangelista	W	7 KO
9/28/79	Las Vegas	Larry Holmes–Earnie Shavers	W	11 KO
10/2/80	Las Vegas	Muhammad Ali–Larry Holmes	L	10 KO
4/11/81	Las Vegas	Larry Holmes–Trevor Berbick	W	15 pts
6/12/81	Detroit	Larry Holmes–Leon Spinks	W	3 KO
12/11/81	Nassau	Muhammad Ali–Trevor Berbick	L	10 pts

Notes

1. Arno Schmidt, *Dark Mirrors,* in *Nobodaddy's Children* (Normal, Ill., 1994), p. 202.
2. Muhammad Ali and Richard Durham, *The Greatest: My Own Story* (New York, 1975), p. 124.
3. Ibid., p. 125.
4. The description in the *New York Times* of 19 June 1963 reads: "Clay, on dream street sixty seconds before, sprang into the center of the ring and laced into Cooper. The first jab snapped Cooper's head back, and opened the eye as a cleaver would have. There were so many punches that Cooper could not have known from whence they were all coming. Cassius was grim, absolutely ruthlessly concentrated. In 2 minutes 15 seconds, he nearly tore Cooper's head off his shoulders. Few men have absorbed such a beating in so short a time. Blood was everywhere. It now was gushing out of Cooper's wounds. Cooper was covering up as best he could. People were screaming, 'Stop the fight!' At last, referee Tommy Little did stop it." In Thomas Hauser, *Muhammad Ali: His Life and Times* (New York, 1991), p. 54.
5. Wilfrid Sheed, *Muhammad Ali: A Portrait in Words and Photographs* (New York, 1975), p. 163.
6. Theodor W. Adorno, *Gesammelte Schriften* (Frankfurt am Main, 1975), vol. 12, p. 137.
7. Thomas Mann, *Felix Krull* (Frankfurt am Main, 1985), p. 298.
8. Ali and Durham, op. cit., p. 123.
9. Randy Roberts, *Papa Jack, Jack Johnson and the Era of White Hopes* (New York, 1983), p. 68

10. *The Odyssey of Homer,* trans. Richard Lattimore (New York, 1965), Book XVIII, ll. 89–99.
11. Christoph Martin Wieland, *Sämtliche Werke* (Leipzig, 1801), vol. 33, p. 20.
12. Hauser, op. cit. p. 305.
13. José Torres, *Sting Like a Bee: The Muhammad Ali Story* (New York, 1971), p. 104.
14. Ali and Durham, op. cit., p. 163.
15. Torres, op. cit., p. 123.
16. Ibid., p. 125.
17. Ibid., p. 127.
18. Ali and Durham, op. cit., p. 119.
19. See Torres, op. cit., p. 142.
20. Ibid., p. 143.
21. Ibid., pp. 145–46.
22. If I have been correctly informed, the Nation of Islam has in the meantime developed into a promoter of "black anti-Semitism," thereby adopting the murderous obsession of its Christian adversary.
23. Torres, op. cit., p. 144.
24. Ibid., p. 149.
25. At this point a boring detail must be inserted. International prizefighting is dominated by two organizations: the WBC (World Boxing Council) and the WBA (World Boxing Association). The WBC is the association that sets the general tone. The rules of the WBA forbid "rematch contracts" (i.e., an agreement requiring a second fight if the title holder should lose). Such a contract existed between Patterson and Liston, but the WBA did not keep a sharp lookout. A similar agreement existed between Liston and Clay. Clay had not made himself well liked, for besides having announced that he was breaking his contract with his (white) Louisville sponsors, he also, as part of his religious conversion, had signed a business contract with the Black Muslims. The WBA took Ali's title away from him and later awarded it to Ernie Terrell.
26. In addition to which, Chuvalo was a member of the WBA, which did not recognize Ali, and therefore Chuvalo could not fight for the world championship. The fight was possible only

because for this fight Ali waived his claim as world champion. His promotional material called him "the People's Champion."

27. The WBA was convinced after the victory over Terrell.

28. Ali and Durham, op. cit., pp. 17 ff.

29. Bill Hughes and Patrick King, eds., *Come Out Writing: A Boxing Anthology* (London, 1991), p. 54.

30. Ibid.

31. Hauser, op. cit., p. 397.

32. Ibid., p. 405.

33. Ibid., pp. 395 ff.

34. Ibid., pp. 412 ff.

35. Ibid., p. 350.

36. Ibid., p. 353.

37. This time (see note 25), it was the WBC that took away the title, because of the rematch with Spinks, thereby refusing to recognize Ali's recapture of the championship. But as was the case with the WBA more than a decade before, the public paid no attention, and the handbooks continue to designate Spinks as world champion. It is very like popes and antipopes. Which organization had proclaimed the right man became clear soon enough.

38. Hauser, op. cit., p. 409.

39. Ibid., pp. 412–13.

40. Ibid., p. 359.

41. John Schulian, *Writers' Fighters and Other Sweet Scientists* (Fairway, Kans., 1983), p. 14; *Sports Illustrated,* 27 February 1978; and the *New York Post,* 16 February 1978.

42. See Jan Philipp Reemtsma, "Clio, oder der Weltprocess" (ms.).

43. Hauser, op. cit., p. 252.

44. Howard Bingham Tape Collection.

45. *Sports Illustrated,* 11 September 1978.

46. Ibid., p. 301.

47. Here we have another allusion to Muhammad Ali, who took on a Japanese wrestler not long after the fight in Manila—an unbelievably embarrassing event.

48. Here, at the very latest, I want to apologize for describing the *Rocky* films without mentioning the supporting role of Paulie, Rocky's brother-in-law, who pops up now and then from the

first film to the last. He sees to it that the films are not totally smothered in pathos and heroism. Paulie is unreliable, grouchy, sometimes mean, always malcontent, and is the only person who does not revere Rocky, but is always dragged along as part of the family, even to Russia. Rocky is fantastic, and Adrian is pretty, but Paulie is the only mensch in the whole circus, the only really lovable character. And in contrast to Sylvester Stallone, who is truly a good actor only in *Rocky I*, Burt Young, who plays Paulie, is one throughout. So, no offense, Paulie!

49. Arno Schmidt, $\frac{B}{M}oondocks$, in *Two Novels* (Normal, Ill., 1998).

50. Ibid.

51. Sigmund Freud, *Moses and Monotheism*, in *The Standard Edition of the Complete Psychological Works of Sigmund Freud*, ed. James Strachey (London, 1964), vol. 23, p. 107.

52. Ibid., p. 125.

53. Hauser, op. cit., pp. 420 ff.

54. Torres, op. cit., p. 128.

55. Ibid., p. 129.

56. Hauser, op. cit., pp. 75 ff.

57. See Peter Fuller, *Champions: The Secret Motives in Games and Sports* (New York, 1976).

58. Hauser, op. cit., p. 76.

59. Ibid., pp. 76 ff.

60. Which argues against the theory of intentional blinding. One can say: *If* Liston's corner had wanted to blind Ali, then Liston would have had to go for broke. Or: The fact that Clay, despite his being blinded, came out at the bell, left Liston uncertain as to whether the attempt had succeeded as planned.

61. Hauser, op. cit., p. 79.

62. Ibid., pp. 78 ff.

63. Norman Mailer, *The Fight* (Boston, 1975), p. 176.

64. Ibid., p. 177.

65. Ibid., pp. 179 ff.

66. Hauser, op. cit., p. 273.

67. Ibid., pp. 275 ff.

68. Ibid., pp. 276 ff.

69. Ibid., pp. 277–78.

70. Mailer, op. cit., p. 195.

71. Ibid., p. 197.

72. Ibid., p. 198.

73. Hauser, op. cit., p. 278.

74. Ibid., p. 326.

75. Ibid., p. 324.

76. For a more extensive discussion, see Jan Philipp Reemtsma, "—und ein Jahrhundert," in *200 Tage und 1 Jahrhundert: Gewalt und Destruktivität im Spiegel des Jahres 1945*, ed. Hamburger Institut für Sozialforschung (Hamburg, 1995).

77. Leo Löwenthal, *Individuum und Terror*, in *Gesammelte Schriften* (Frankfurt am Main, 1982), vol. 3, p. 161.

78. See Sheed, op. cit.

79. All of Muhammad Ali's fights as a professional boxer are listed here, but only the most interesting ones of his opponents, and of these latter only such as have a bearing on their status as Ali's opponents.

Bibliography

Adorno, Theodor W. *Gesammelte Schriften.* Edited by Rolf Tiede-
    mann. Frankfurt am Main, 1972.

Ali, Muhammad, and Richard Durham. *The Greatest: My Own
    Story.* New York, 1975.

Andre, Sam, and Nat Fleischer. *A Pictorial History of Boxing.*
    London, 1988.

Berger, Phil. *Blood Season.* London, 1989.

Bloch, Ernst. *Gesammelte Werke.* Frankfurt am Main, 1969.

Freud, Sigmund. *The Standard Edition of the Complete Psycho-
    logical Works of Sigmund Freud.* Edited by James Strachey.
    London, 1964.

Fuller, Peter. *Champions: The Secret Motives in Games and Sports.*
    New York, 1976.

Hails, Jack. *Classic Moments of Boxing.* Ashbourne, 1989.

Haskins, James. *Sugar Ray Leonard.* New York, 1989.

Hauser, Thomas. *Muhammad Ali: His Life and Times.* New York,
    1991.

Hughes, Bill, and Patrick King, eds. *Come Out Writing: A Boxing
    Anthology.* London, 1991.

Jones, Ken, and Chris Smith. *Boxing: The Champions.* Swindon,
    1990.

Kent, Graeme. *Boxing's Strangest Fights.* London, 1991.

Leifer, Neil, and Thomas Hauser. *Muhammad Ali Memories.* New
    York, 1992.

Mailer, Norman. *The Fight.* Boston, 1975.

Manthey, Dirk, and Jörg Altendorf, eds. *Sylvester Stallone.* New York, 1990.

Morrison, Ian. *Boxing: The Records.* Enfield, 1988.

———. *Boxing's Who's Who.* Enfield, 1992.

Oates, Joyce Carol. *On Boxing.* New York, 1987.

Schmidt, Arno. *Collected Early Fiction, 1949–1964.* 4 vols. Translated by John E. Woods. Normal, Ill., 1994–98.

Sheed, Wilfrid. *Muhammad Ali: A Portrait in Words and Photographs.* New York, 1975.

Sugar, Randolph. *The Great Fights: A Pictorial History of Boxing's Greatest Bouts.* New York, n.d.

Torres, José. *Fire and Fear: The Inside Story of Mike Tyson.* New York, 1989.

———. *Sting Like a Bee: The Muhammad Ali Story.* New York, 1971.

Wiley, Ralph. *Serenity: A Boxing Quest from Sugar Ray Robinson to Mike Tyson.* Edinburgh, 1989.

A Note About the Author

Jan Philipp Reemtsma was born in Germany in 1952. A philologist by training, he is the director of both the Hamburg Institute for Social Research and the Arno Schmidt Foundation. He lives in Hamburg.

A Note About the Translator

John E. Woods is the distinguished translator of many books—most notably Arno Schmidt's *Evening Edged in Gold,* for which he won both the American Book Award for translation and the PEN Translation Prize in 1981; Patrick Süskind's *Perfume,* for which he again won the PEN Translation Prize, in 1987; Christoph Ransmayr's *The Terrors of Ice and Darkness, The Last World* (for which he was awarded the Schlegel-Tieck Prize in 1991), and *The Dog King;* and Thomas Mann's *Buddenbrooks, The Magic Mountain,* and, most recently, *Doctor Faustus.* For his translations of *The Magic Mountain* and Arno Schmidt's *Nobodaddy's Children,* he was presented the first Helen and Kurt Wolff Prize for Translation from the German in 1996. Mr. Woods lives in San Diego.

A Note on the Type

This book was set in Caledonia, a typeface designed by W. A. Dwiggins (1880–1956). It belongs to the family of printing types called "modern face" by printers—a term used to mark the change in style of the type letters that occurred around 1800. Caledonia borders on the general design of Scotch Roman but it is more freely drawn than that letter.

Composed by Stratford Publishing Services, Inc.,
Brattleboro, Vermont
Printed and bound by R. R. Donnelley & Sons,
Harrisonburg, Virginia
Designed by Anthea Lingeman